The
OREGON
COAST GUIDE

MIKE & KRISTY WESTBY

ISBN-13: 978-0998395098

072318

*"The sea, once it casts its spell,
holds one in its net of wonder forever."*

Jacques Cousteau

FOLLOW
DISCOVER-OREGON

Yaquina Head Lighthouse

On the Web:
www.Discover-Oregon.com

On Twitter:
@DiscoverOre.com

On Facebook:
www.Facebook.com/DiscoverORE

On Instagram:
DiscoverOregon4300

THE
OREGON COAST GUIDE

Haystack Rock – Pacific City

The Oregon Coast is filled with an abundance of scenic and cultural attractions. Long sandy beaches offer sweeping panoramic vistas, steam-like spouts reveal passing Gray Whales, while tide pools hide tiny creatures scurrying from view. Inland, majestic lighthouses illuminate the history of the coast and its inhabitants, a coastal town holds its annual sandcastle building contest, and steam trains, dune buggies and jet boats all provide a thrill of a lifetime!

With *so many* destinations and attractions, how do you begin to discover what to see and do when you visit the coast? The answer...**The Oregon Coast Guide**. We've listed over 200 attractions for you to visit, complete with descriptions, contact information, hours, tips and usually a photo or two, so you can just pick your destination on the Oregon Coast and then open this guide to instantly discover an abundance of things to see and do while you're there!

Enjoy your trip!

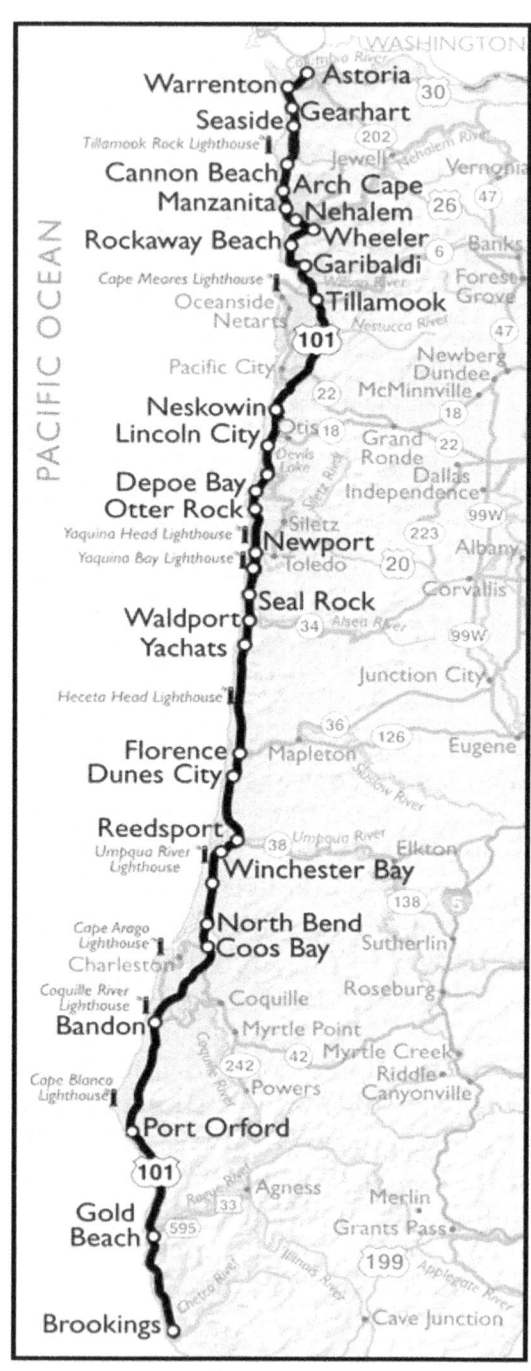

Map Courtesy of www.TravelOregon.com

WHERE TO GO

HOW TO USE THIS GUIDE

Shore Acres State Park

You may use this guide in two different ways...

Choose Your Oregon Coast Destination - Pick a destination, such as Newport, Cape Perpetua, or the Three Capes Scenic Drive, and then open this book to check out all of the sites you can visit at your destination for the day, weekend, or longer.

Or

Choose Your Oregon Coast Activity - Flip through the pages of *The Oregon Coast Guide*, choose which activities you'd like to experience, and then head on out! Want to try your luck crabbing for fresh Dungeness crabs? Then head to Kelly's Brighton Marina in Rockaway Beach. Want to ride in the cab of a old-fashioned steam locomotive? Then you'll be looking to ride the Oregon Coast Scenic Railroad in Garibaldi. Or maybe you want to watch powerful waves crashing against the shore during a winter storm. If that's the case, then you'll be making your way to Shore Acres State Park. Find what excites your adventurous spirit and explore the Oregon Coast!

North to South

Generally, the attractions and some of the scenic drives in The Oregon Coast Guide are listed in a north to south orientation, beginning with Astoria in the north and finishing with Brookings in the south, but it all works south to north, too!

Timing

The Oregon Coast is a beautiful destination any time of the year, with the conditions changing dramatically from season to season. Spring, summer and fall bring some of the finest weather in Oregon, as well as the entire United States, while winter can produce brooding or stormy skies, perfect for watching waves explode at Cape Kiwanda, enjoying a bowl of warm clam chowder by a window in a small restaurant, or simply reading a book in your hotel room while under a blanket beside a warm fire.

They're Your Beaches

In 1967, Oregon passed what is known as *The Beach Bill*, and this declared that all of Oregon's beaches belong to the public. As a result, none of Oregon's beaches are privately owned, and all visitors to the Oregon Coast may enjoy any and all of Oregon's beautiful beaches without restriction.

Whale Watching

You can expect to see some whales during your trip, as nearly 20,000 gray whales migrate up and down the coast year-round, with most being spotted from mid-December through January, from late March to June, and then through the summer months, with September being a high point of the year. Fortunately, most of the destinations you visit in this book, such as Cape

Lookout, Cape Perpetua, Yaquina Head, and many others, are perfect for spotting whales. See the article titled *Whale Watching on the Oregon Coast* on Page 157 to learn more about this exciting and memorable Oregon tradition.

COASTAL PARKING PERMITS

Some of the more popular Oregon State Parks, Recreation Areas, Trail Heads, Scenic Areas, etc. charge a parking fee, and this varies from $5 for a daily permit, to $35 for an annual permit, depending upon the type of permit purchased. Note that some non-annual permits are valid for five to seven days, so they may be used at multiple sites during your visit to the coast.

Oregon State Parks Day-Use Parking Permit – Daily: $5 – Annual: $30 – This permit is honored at all 26 Oregon State Parks that charge a parking fee. Permits are available at self-service kiosks, park booths, or offices located at the site in which a permit is required. In addition, they may be purchased by calling 800-551-6949. If you're camping, you do not need a parking permit. Just display your current state park camping receipt on your dashboard.

Oregon Pacific Coast Passport – 5-Day Permit: $10.00 – Annual Permit: $35.00. A day use permit that covers vehicle parking and day use fees for over 15 sites along Hwy 101, (the Pacific Coast Scenic Byway) including Shore Acres, Cape Lookout, Yaquina Head Outstanding Natural Area, Heceta Head and more. Available for purchase at sites along the coast, as well as by calling 800-551-6949.

Bring Your Binoculars

From sweeping panoramic vistas and off shore sea stacks to lazing seals and passing whales, there is much to see during your Oregon Coast visit, and a good pair of binoculars will bring much of it closer to  you, so be sure to bring a pair along when you visit the coast.

Take Your Time and Enjoy The Sights

 As you make your way through this book, you'll see a small clock icon placed next to some of the listings. There are many Oregon Coast attractions that do not require much time to visit. A stop at The Olde Telephone Company in Newport may require about half an hour, while a stop at Simpson Beach to see the hundreds of seals on the rocks may require half that, but locations and attractions such as Cape Perpetua, Oswald West State Park, Yaquina Head Lighthouse and the Oregon Coast Scenic Railway absolutely call for you to spend more time enjoying the commanding views or once-in-a-lifetime experiences. Wherever you see the clock icon within these pages, plan on spending at least an hour at that location, and we would encourage you to spend even more time there while enjoying the view, walking the beach or even piloting a boat while catching fresh Dungeness crabs.

www.Discover-Oregon.com

Astoria, Fort Stevens, Warrenton, Gearhart, Seaside & Cannon Beach

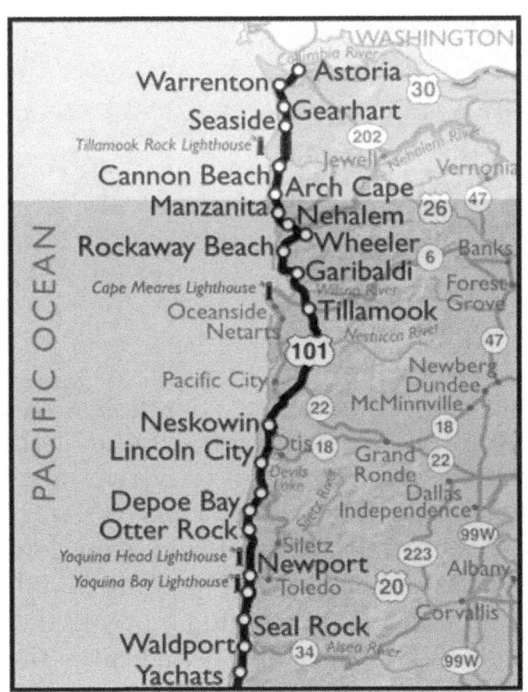

Astoria, OR

Located in the northwest corner of the state, Astoria is a vibrant town rich in history, with much of it tied to the fishing industry and the bounty of the Pacific Ocean. Make a reservation for a Friday and Saturday night at one of the historic hotels in town and spend the weekend exploring Astoria's past. Walk, bicycle or ride a trolley along the Astoria Riverwalk and learn about how Astoria's history is inextricably tied to both the mighty Columbia River and the Pacific Ocean, climb the Astoria Column for an amazing view of the city, (and to try your balsa wood airplane piloting prowess!) wander through the Flavel House Museum to get a sense of life in days past, and make your way to the Fort Clatsop & Lewis and Clark NHP to learn about the lives of these early explorers in the Pacific Northwest.

☐ Astoria Riverwalk

 Covering 6.4 miles along the Columbia River is the Astoria Riverwalk. Formerly an old rail line, today it has been converted into a level paved pathway that allows visitors to stroll or bike their way beneath the towering Astoria-  Megler bridge and past restaurants, antique shops, gift shops, cannery museums, breweries, river viewpoints, docks with barking sea lions, and more. It's a perfect way to reach the Columbia River Maritime Museum and experience the active river front area of Astoria. And if you are walking instead of riding a bike, and you feel like taking a break, then hop aboard "Old 300", a colorful 1913 trolley which plys the tracks from noon to 6:00 p.m. along the Riverwalk every day, depending upon the weather. For only $1, you can hop aboard, sit down, relax and take in the sights. For only $2, you can hop on and

off all day as much as you'd like. Note that you can ride the trolley round-trip, which takes about one hour.

Tip: If you're staying at the Cannery Pier Hotel, then inquire about borrowing their bikes for a casual yet speedy way to enjoy the Riverwalk.

☐ Columbia River Maritime Museum

Located on the Astoria Riverwalk next to the Columbia River is the modern Columbia River Maritime Museum, recognized as one of the finest museums in the state. Filled with dramatic displays and interactive exhibits, the museum allows visitors to learn all about the legendary Columbia River Bar. Here, the powerful force of the mighty Columbia River meets the strength of the even mightier Pacific Ocean to create one of the most dangerous passages in the world, one in which vessels large and small must at times navigate waves reaching 40' in height during fierce winter storms. Docked nearby is the Columbia Lightship, which was stationed as a floating lighthouse 5.2 statute miles from the mouth of the Columbia River from 1951 to 1979. Visitors are welcome to board and tour the vessel as part of the museum experience.

Columbia River Maritime Museum
1792 Marine Drive
Astoria, OR 97103
503-325-2323

- Open Monday through Friday – 9:30 a.m. to 5:00 p.m.
- Admission: Adults: $14.00 – Seniors: $12.00 – Children 6 and over: $5.00.

☐ The Astoria Column

Towering 125' atop 600' high Coxcomb Hill in Astoria is the colorful Astoria Column. Built in 1926 and one of Oregon's most visited parks, the column rewards those who climb its 164 steps with a commanding view of Astoria, Young's Bay, the Astoria-Megler Bridge, the Coast Range, the Columbia River and the Pacific Ocean. And just for fun, aspiring pilots, young and old, wishing to try their skills can purchase a balsa wood airplane at the column's gift shop, climb the stairs, and launch their craft into the wild blue yonder. Will it make it all the way to the Washington side of the Columbia River...or just to the parking lot below?

The Astoria Column
1 Coxcomb Drive
Astoria, OR 97103
503-325-2963

- The Astoria Column is open from dawn to dusk.
- The Gift Shop is open Monday through Sunday – 9:00 a.m. to 7:00 p.m.
- There is no charge to visit the column, though parking is $5 per vehicle.

www.Discover-Oregon.com

☐ Flavel House Museum

One of the finest examples of Queen Anne architecture in Oregon, as well as the Pacific Northwest, the 1886 Captain George Flavel House and surrounding grounds take up an entire lot at the corner of 8th and Duane Street. Impressive in its time, as well  as today, this 11,600 square-foot 2½ story home welcomes visitors with an abundance of grand rooms, all expertly decorated with high-quality period-specific furnishings, amenities and wood work. Being a museum, tours are offered in which visitors can roam about the home while learning about Captain George Flavel, a Bar Pilot on the Columbia River and one of Astoria's most influential citizens during the late 1800s.

Tickets for tours are available in the carriage house, located at the corner of 7th & Exchange Streets, at the southwest corner of the lot. Here, visitors can also watch a short orientation video about the home before embarking on their tour.

> Flavel House Museum
> 441 8th Street
> Astoria, OR 97103
> 503-325-2203

> • Open Monday through Sunday – 11:00 a.m. to 4:00 p.m.

☐ Oregon Film Museum

Oregon has been the filming location for many famous movies, and these are celebrated at the Oregon Film Museum. Housed in the old 1914 Clatsop County Jail, you'll find tributes to The

Goonies, Animal House, One Flew Over the Cuckoo's Nest, The Shining, Paint Your Wagon, Stand by Me, and many others.

Oregon Film Museum
732 Duane Street
Astoria, OR 97103
503-325-2203

Hours & Admission:

- $6 Adults, $2 Children 6 - 17
- May - Sept.: Monday through Sunday - 10:00 a.m. to 5:00 p.m.
- Oct. - April: Monday through Sunday - 11:00 a.m. to 4:00 p.m.

☐ Heritage Museum

Housed in a charming 1904 building which used to serve as Astoria's City Hall, the Heritage Museum allows visitors to explore the rich history of Astoria and Clatsop County, with exhibits featuring Native Americans of this area, early Pioneers, the logging, fishing and canning industries that were so important to Astoria, and the immigrants that arrived to work the difficult jobs in the forests, canneries and at sea. In addition, visitors can learn about the construction of Highway 101 and the campaign to build the Astoria-Megler Bridge.

Heritage Museum
1618 Exchange Street
Astoria, OR 97103
503-338-4849

- Open Monday through Sunday - 10:00 a.m. to 5:00 p.m.

☐ Museum of Whimsy

An eclectic and artistic collection of items assembled within two floors of a neo-classic bank building from the 1920s. Stop in to discover the "curious, whimsical, and fantastic".

Museum of Whimsy
1215 Duane Street
Astoria, OR 97103
425-417-6512

- Admission: $ 5 Per person - $10 Per family
- Open Friday through Sunday – 11:00 a.m. to 5:00 p.m.

☐ Astoria Sunday Market

Stroll among over 100 vendors offering locally "grown, crafted and gathered" fares and wares at the Astoria Sunday Market, the second largest market of its kind in Oregon. Have lunch at the lively food court and enjoy some live music.

Astoria Sunday Market
12th Street
Astoria, OR 97103
503-325-1010

- Open Sundays – 10:00 a.m. to 3:00 p.m. - From Mother's Day in May through the second Sunday in October

www.Discover-Oregon.com

☐ Fort Clatsop & Lewis and Clark NHP

Step back in time with a visit to a replica of Fort Clatsop, where Lewis and Clark, as part of the Corps of Discovery, spent the long and difficult winter of 1805 to 1806 before embarking on their return journey back east to St. Louis.

Lewis and Clark NHP
92343 Fort Clatsop Road
Astoria, OR 97103
503-861-2471

- Open daily 9:00 a.m. to 6:00 p.m. – Late June to September, 9:00 a.m. to 5:00 p.m. during the winter.

FORT STEVENS - WARRENTON - HAMMOND, OR

 ☐ **Fort Stevens State Park**

Located at the mouth of the Columbia River is historic Fort Stevens. Initially built in 1865 to protect this important waterway from Confederate gun boats and the British Navy during the Civil War, it continued to serve in this role during the Spanish-American

War, World War I and World War II. Today, the shadows and stories of its past are preserved for visitors as part of a 4,300 acre State Park offering a military museum, massive concrete

artillery gun batteries, historic structures, Civil War reenactments, and an information center. In addition, visitors will find an abundance of recreational activities, including camping, hiking, wildlife viewing, biking and more. A favorite among visitors is a walk out on the ocean shore, where they will discover the rusting skeletal remains of the Peter Iredale, a four-masted sailing ship that ran ashore in 1906.

Note that tours of Fort Stevens are available by contacting the Friends of Old Fort Stevens at 503-861-2000.

Fort Stevens State Park
100 Peter Iredale Road
Hammond, OR 97121
800-551-6949

- Open: Daily – 6:00 a.m. to 10:00 p.m.

 ☐ **High Life Adventures**

Experience the high-flying adventure of a guided 8-line zip line tour through an Oregon Coast forest up to 75' in the air!

- Flights take 2 to 2.5 Hours
- Adult: (16 and older) $99
- Child: (15 and under) $69
- Some weight restrictions apply
- It's best to call and make reservations 1 day in advance for mid-week flights, and 2 days in advance for weekends. However, walk-ons may also be available.

High Life Adventures
92111 High Life Road
Warrenton, OR 97146
503-861-9875

- Open: Daily - 10:00 a.m. to 8:00 p.m., Closed Tuesday and Wednesday during the winter.

SEASIDE, OR

If you're looking for a busy seaside resort town filled with many fun and different boardwalk-like activities, then you're looking for Seaside, Oregon. Punctuated by a main drag that funnels cars to a turnaround on the prom overlooking a broad sandy beach that goes on forever, Seaside offers families a generous mix of seaside activities, including indoor bumper cars, go-carts, miniature golf, paddle boats, bike rentals for a ride on the sand, Oregon's largest arcade, the Seaside Aquarium, an indoor mall with a colorful carousel, corn dogs, cotton candy and over 100 flavors of an Oregon Coast favorite...salt water taffy!

☐ Explore Seaside and the Beach by Bike

Whether taking the family out on a "bicycle" surrey built for four, exploring on a tandem, or taking to the sand on a three-wheeled "Beach Cruiser", you'll have a blast exploring Seaside and the beach by bike. Stop in at a local shop and rent a ride by the hour.

- Prom Bike Shop – 622 12th Ave., Seaside, OR 97138 – 503-738-8251

- Wheel Fun Rentals – 407 S. Holladay Dr., Seaside, OR 97138 – 503-738-8447

- Wheel Fun Rentals – 151 Avenue A, Seaside, OR 97138 – 503-738-7212

www.Discover-Oregon.com

☐ Seaside Aquarium

Founded in 1937, the privately owned Seaside Aquarium is one of the oldest aquariums on the west coast. Inside, visitors will find interpretive exhibits, touch tanks and a collection of crabs, Wolf Eels, Ling Cod, star fish, a Giant Pacific Octopus, and of course seals, for which the aquarium is known.

Admission:

Adults:	$8.50
Children 6 – 13:	$4.25 (Children 5 and under are free)
Seniors 64+:	$7.25
Family – Up to 6:	$29.00

Seaside Aquarium
200 N Prom
Seaside, OR 97138
503-738-6211

- Open Daily 9:00 a.m. until closing, which varies.

☐ Funland Arcade

Visit the Funland Arcade and be greeted by an impressive collection of hundreds of arcade games, from the latest challenges to some of your favorite classics. In addition, you'll find boardwalk games, bumper cars, pizza and more.

Funland Arcade
201 Broadway
Seaside, OR 97138
503-738-5612

- Open 9:00 a.m. to 10:00 p.m. – Sunday through Thursday, 9:00 a.m. to 11:00 p.m. – Friday and Saturday

☐ Seaside Historical Society Museum

Step inside the Seaside Historical Society Museum to learn about Seaside's history as a resort town beginning in the late 1800s, including its interesting historical attractions, its busy boardwalk, the industries of the area, the Seaside Railroad, and more. In addition, tour the Butterfield Cottage and its gardens, which accurately depict a Seaside cottage in the year of 1912.

Seaside Museum & Historical Society
570 Necanicum Dr.
Seaside, OR 97138
503-738-7065

- Open Monday through Sat. – 10:00 a.m. to 3:00 p.m.

☐ Seaside Helicopter Tours

Your trip to the Oregon Coast can take to the air! Choose from a selection of different helicopter tours to see Seaside, Cannon Beach and Oregon's north coast from high in the sky.

Seaside Helicopter, LLC.
2665 South Roosevelt Drive
85913 US-101
Seaside, OR 97138
503-440-4123

Tour of Seaside: $50 Per person (3 Seat minimum) – Cannon Beach: $109 (2 Seat minimum) – Reservations are not required.

Open: Monday through Sunday – 12:00 p.m. to 6:00 p.m. Memorial Day Weekend through October. Hours are weather dependent, and they're open other times of the year, as well, including Spring Break in March and occasionally in winter.

☐ Captain Kid Amusement Park

Seaside wouldn't be Seaside without bumper cars, go-carts, and mini-golf, and you'll find each of these at the Captain Kid Amusement Park. Bring the family and have some laughs!

Captain Kid Amusement Park
2735 S Roosevelt Dr.
85883 Highway 101
Seaside, OR 97138
503-738-2076

* Open

  * Summer: Saturday through Monday – 11:00 a.m. to 6:00 p.m.
  * Winter: Daily – 11:00 a.m. to 6:00 p.m.

Note: Captain Kid Amusement Park is located immediately south of Seaside Helicopter Tours, ¼ mile south of Seaside.

CANNON BEACH, OR

Voted one of the World's 100 Most Beautiful Places by National Geographic, Cannon Beach is a charming seaside town filled with a collection of shops, boutiques, art galleries, bookstores, glass blowing studios, restaurants, quaint beach cottages and more. In addition, it offers a broad sandy beach for strolling, as well as iconic Haystack Rock. Rising 235 feet above the ocean waves, it is home to colorful Tufted Puffins, as well as other ocean birds, and offers access to fascinating tide pools at low tide. See the next page for additional details.

 ☐ **Ecola State Park**

Found just north of Cannon Beach is scenic Ecola State Park. Here, multiple trails offer stunning views of the Pacific Ocean, secluded coves, Cannon Beach, and the abandoned Tillamook Rock Lighthouse, located on a ½ acre of rock 1.2 miles out into the ocean from  Tillamook Head. Note that a $5 Day Use permit is required to park at Ecola State Park, and permits may be purchased at the fee station on the drive into the park.

Hikes:

- Ecola Point to Indian Beach Hike – 1.5 Miles – Easy
- Clatsop Loop Hike – 3 Miles – 700' gain – Easy
- Crescent Beach Hike – 3.6 Miles – 310' of elevation gain – Moderate

☐ **Icefire Glassworks**

Located across the street from The Cannon Beach Hotel is Icefire Glassworks, a working glass studio offering colorful works of glass art for sale, as well as close up views of glass artist James Kingwell skillfully practicing his craft.

Icefire Glassworks
116 E Gower Ave.
Cannon Beach, OR 97110
503-436-2359

- Open: Monday through Sunday – 10:00 a.m. to 5:00 p.m. – Closed Tuesdays and Wednesdays in the winter.

☐ Haystack Rock

One of the most iconic landmarks in all of Oregon, Haystack Rock at Cannon Beach stands as a towering force against the tides and torrents of the Pacific Ocean. Rising 235 feet above the waves, it beckons tourists to explore its ever-changing tide pools and discover colorful sea stars, anemones, sea urchins, crabs and more, all as one of Oregon's seven designated Marine Gardens. High on its rocky perches, visitors will find an abundance of birdlife, including the Pelagic Cormorant, Black Oystercatcher, Harlequin Ducks, the Pigeon Guillemot and colorful Tufted Puffins, which can be spotted during the early spring to mid-summer months, with the best times being early April to mid-May and late June through July.

Note:

- There are two Haystack Rocks on the Oregon coast. You'll find another at Pacific City.

- To visit the tide pools, plan to arrive at Haystack Rock at least one hour before low tide. Weather and low tides permitting, you'll often find naturalists on the beach throughout the year offering a wealth of interpretive information about the tide pools, as well as the sea life and birds that inhabit the rock.

- Always practice beach safety when exploring the tide pools. Know if the tide is coming in or going out, and *never turn your back on the ocean*, as a "sneaker wave" can come at any time to sweep you or a loved one from the rocks.

☐ Cannon Beach History Center & Museum

Stop in at the Cannon Beach History Center & Museum to learn about the history of Cannon Beach and the interesting story of how the town got its name. In addition, take a moment to peruse through their interesting collection of over 12,000 historical photos.

Cannon Beach History Center and Museum
1387 S. Spruce Street
Cannon Beach, OR 97110
503-436-9301

- Open Wednesday through Monday – 11:00 a.m. to 4:00 p.m.

☐ Cannon Beach Sandcastle Contest

Cannon Beach is a small yet busy seaside town year-round, but during one weekend each Spring, the town bursts at its seams with its largest crowds of the year during the Cannon Beach Sandcastle Contest. Pros, amateurs, groups, families, and other artisans skilled in crafting works of art from sand compete for awards in numerous categories as crowds of visitors look on in amazement at what they have sculpted. It's all part of a weekend long event that includes parades, a 5K fun run and walk, music, a beach bonfire, and more.

Note that this event is high and low tide dependent, so a decision is made each year as to when a Saturday in late May to mid-June offers the best conditions for building sand castles. For the latest information, call the Cannon Beach Chamber of Commerce at 503-436-2623 or visit www.CannonBeach.org

Generally speaking, hotel reservations should be made at least 6 months in advance, and those arriving for just the day should arrive early.

☐ Cannon Beach Farmers Market

Walk over to the Cannon Beach Farmers Market from nearby downtown Cannon Beach's shopping area and you'll find a collection of hand-crafted goods, colorful flowers, and artisan food products, including fresh produce, organic cheeses, local berries,  baked items, seafood and more, all produced by local farmers, ranchers, and fishermen.

Cannon Beach Farmers Market
163 E Grower Ave.
Cannon Beach, OR 97110

- Open Tuesdays – 1:00 p.m. to 5:00 p.m.- Mid-June to late September

☐ Cannon Beach Cottage & Garden Tour

 As a tourist destination and "sportsman's paradise" since the late 1800s, Cannon Beach is filled with countless small cottages. Crafted with a historical look, vintage charm, or architectural styling, each cottage welcomes its visitors with creative and colorful landscaping, and a unique coastal sense of character.

Every September, Cannon Beach celebrates its cottages with its annual Cottage & Garden Tour. Part of a weekend long event filled with interesting lectures, an English style garden tea, live music and more, visitors can enjoy strolling through town on a self-guided tour as they admire the gardens, steal an idea or two, and walk through the cottages as a welcome guest.

Maps are handed out at the start of the tour and are your ticket inside each home. Contact the Cannon Beach History Center and Museum for additional information at www.CBHistory.org

☐ Bruce's Candy Kitchen

Just north of Tom's Fish & Chips in Cannon Beach, which serves excellent fish & chips and more, by the way, is Bruce's Candy Kitchen. They sell all kinds of candy, including some old-fashioned and hard to find varieties, but if you've ever wondered how they wrap all of those pieces of salt water taffy, then you'll want to step inside to see the automated salt water taffy machine clicking along as it cuts and wraps thousands of pieces of taffy at a time!

Bruce's Candy Kitchen
256 N Hemlock St.
Cannon Beach, OR 97110

Oswald West State Park, Manzanita, Wheeler, Rockaway Beach, Garibaldi & Tillamook

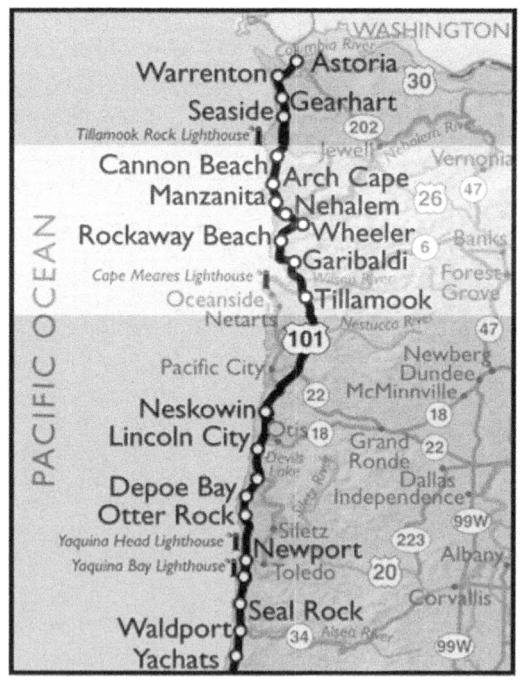

OSWALD WEST STATE PARK

 ☐ **Oswald West State Park - Hike to Short Sand Beach**

Of the hikes we've done on the Oregon Coast, this one rates in the Top 10 for us. In fact, Kristy says it's one of her Top three favorite picnic spots on the entire coast, with the other two being at Cape Perpetua and the Umpqua Lighthouse.

Park in the large (and busy in the summer) parking lot and take the trail at the north end of the lot under Hwy 101. (Watch your head!) Hike ½ mile on the broad and largely smooth trail to Short Sand Beach. Here, you can walk the short beach, explore a small (and short) cave on the north end at low tide, and watch surfers practice in the waves. Note: There are three picnic tables and three benches for enjoying the view. You'll find restrooms in the parking lot, as well.

MANZANITA & NEHALEM, OR

☐ **Manzanita, Oregon**

Manzanita is one of those great small coastal towns with a strong sense of community. Stroll along Laneda Avenue and enjoy the restaurants, shops, boutiques, bookstores, candy shops and more before making your way just a short distance to Manzanita's long and beautiful sandy beach, anchored by Nehalem Bay State Park on the south and Neah-Kah-Nie Mountain on the north. Note: With easy access from town, Nehalem Bay State Park offers some excellent paved bike paths.

☐ Manzanita Farmers Market

A small yet popular farmers market showcases handmade crafts, fresh produce, fresh baked goods, photography, and more from local farms, orchards, wineries, and artisans, all with live music.

Located in the City parking lot at 5th Street South & Laneda Avenue in Manzanita, OR.

Open: Summer Hours: Fridays 5:00 p.m. to 8:00 p.m. – Early June to late August. The hours shift one hour earlier in the day during September before closing for the winter months.

☐ Nehalem, Oregon

Spanning both sides of Highway 101, Nehalem is a quaint beach town welcoming travelers to stop and visit. Stop in to peruse some shops, find an antique or two, and enjoy a treat at Buttercup Handmade Ice Cream and Chowders.

35915 N Hwy 101
Nehalem, OR 97131
503-368-2469

- Open Wednesday through Sunday – 11:30 a.m. to 6:00 p.m.

WHEELER, OR

☐ **Wheeler, Oregon**

As with Nehalem, Wheeler, Oregon welcomes visitors with a small collection of shops. Visit the Old Wheeler Hotel, which has been very nicely renovated in period-specific detail, and ask if you may have a quick tour as a reference for your future stays at the coast.

Old Wheeler Hotel
495 Hwy 101
Wheeler, OR 97147
503-368-6000

 ☐ **Oregon Coast Railriders**

Just as with their location a little ways south in Bay City, Oregon Coast Railriders offers an adventurous "railriding" excursion out of Wheeler, Oregon. Make your way along the Nehalem River as you pedal through the dense forests and unique views of the Oregon Coast mountain range before returning back to Wheeler.

Note: Plan on arriving 30 minutes before your departure to sign in, be assigned a railcar, and load. Most round-trips take approximately 2 hours and 45 minutes total. Departures occur at 9:00 a.m., 12:00 noon and 3:00 p.m. on Saturday through Wednesday. See page 42 for additional details.

ROCKAWAY BEACH, OR

 ☐ **Kelly's Brighton Marina**

You can't have the Oregon Coast without Dungeness crab, and you can't have Dungeness crab without going crabbing!

There are a number of places along the Oregon Coast where you can go crabbing, and we recommend three within this guide. The first you'll come across is Kelly's Brighton Marina, just south of Wheeler, OR and Nehalem Bay. Bustling with families, campers, and road trippers on a summer's day, Kelly's Brighton Marina welcomes crabbers of all kinds, be they salty seasoned pros or novices visiting the ocean for their very first time. Kelly himself will see to it that you learn everything you need to know to catch, cook, clean and eat a crab, all while having fun doing it. In fact, he promises you'll have a blast!

If you haven't been crabbing before, here's the process...

- Rent some crab rings, bait, and a nice clean motorboat from Kelly's Brighton Marina. It's $95 for 2 hours and $25 for each additional hour. For this, you'll receive a boat and motor, 3 baited crab rings, safety gear, and the cooking of any legal sized crabs you catch. (You *must* return any females or less than legal sized crabs to the water.)

- Head out into the bay (not the ocean!) and drop your crab rings into the water. Pull them up periodically to see what you've caught. Return to shore with your legal crabs and have Kelly's cook them up for you. Cooking the crabs takes 20 to 30 minutes.

- Clean your crabs and then find a picnic table outside Kelly's with a view of the bay and enjoy this delectable taste of Oregon with a plate, utensils and shell cracker provided as part of your boat rental fee.

As an option to renting a boat, you may rent a crab ring and crab off of Kelly's dock. For $12, you'll receive a crab ring with the first round of bait, access to the dock, and cooking of any legal sized crabs. The dock closes at 5:00 p.m. or one hour before dark, whichever is earlier.

Note: If you do not have an Oregon annual shellfish license, you'll need buy one here for $7.00.

Kelly's Brighton Marina
29200 US-101
Rockaway Beach, OR 97136
503-368-5745

- Open Monday through Sunday – 6:00 a.m. to 6:30 p.m.

☐ International Police Museum

Stop in to see an interesting small museum dedicated to preserving the culture, history and heritage of the Rockaway Beach and Oregon police departments. You'll find many national and international departments represented here, as well.

International Police Museum
216 US-101
Rockaway Beach, OR 97136

- Open Monday through Friday – 10:00 a.m. to 4:00 p.m.

☐ The Original Pronto Pup

You've had them at carnivals, state fairs and ballgames, but did you know that corndogs were invented right here, in Rockaway Beach, Oregon? Stop in at the Original Pronto Pup and enjoy a taste of history. When you're finished, take a ride on the world's first Riding Mechanical Corndog, just outside the restaurant.

Pronto Pup
602 US-101
Rockaway Beach, OR 97136
971-306-1164

- Open Thursday through Saturday – 11:00 a.m. to 7:00 p.m., Sundays 11:00 a.m. to 4:00 p.m. – Closed Monday through Thursday from October until Memorial Day.

GARIBALDI, OR

Located at the northern end of Tillamook Bay, Garibaldi is a small town with a busy marina offering fresh seafood and good restaurants. In addition, it's here that you'll board the Oregon Coast Scenic Railroad for a journey back in time.

The Oregon Coast Scenic Railroad

Journey back in time to the era of steam aboard the Oregon Coast Scenic Railroad. Climb aboard the vintage railcars, pulled by a massive 1925 steam locomotive, and journey north for 45 minutes from Garibaldi, OR to Rockaway Beach, OR. Along the way, you'll parallel Garibaldi Bay, ride along forested tracks, and pass through coastal neighborhoods before pulling into Rockaway, where you'll have 30 minutes to disembark and walk the nearby beach, explore some shops, and, of course, buy some saltwater taffy. Then, you'll reboard the steam train and enjoy your 45 minute return journey back to Garibaldi.

Note: For a truly unique Oregon Coast experience, make a reservation to ride in the cab of the locomotive for your round-trip journey. You'll get an up close look at the engine, be able to ask questions of the Engineer and Fireman, and, if you're lucky, actually pull the cord to blow the steam whistle! Make your reservations online before arriving.

Pricing:

Adults – 11 to 61 Years Old:	$20
Seniors – 62+ Years Old:	$18
Veterans – With Military ID:	$18
Children – 3 to 10 Years Old:	$12
Children Under 3 Years Old:	Free
Cab Rides – Per Person:	$52

Note: Tickets, once purchased, are non-refundable, but may be used to reschedule a similar excursion within the same year.

Tickets:

Tickets may be purchased in the caboose when you arrive at the station. Reservations for rides in the cab should be made online prior to your arrival, but may also be made after you arrive if space is available.

Schedule:

- Departing Garibaldi: 10:00 a.m., 12:00 p.m. & 2:00 p.m.

- Departing Rockaway Beach: 11:00 a.m. & 1:00 p.m.

Oregon Coast Scenic Railroad
402 American Avenue
Garibaldi, OR 97118
503-842-7972

☐ Garibaldi Maritime Museum

Stop in at the Garibaldi Maritime Museum to learn all about the voyages of Captain Robert Gray. Inside, you'll discover models of his ships, the Lady Washington and the Columbia Rediviva, as well as countless historical seafaring items including a partially completed 18th century transport boat, an eight foot tall reproduction of the Columbia's figurehead, a half-model depicting how his ships were provisioned for long voyages to the Pacific Northwest, and much more. This is a very interesting and well-curated museum.

Admission:

- $4.00 – 11 and older, $3.00 – Seniors 62 and over
- Children 10 and younger are free

Open:

- April through October: Thursday through Monday – 10:00 a.m. to 4:00 p.m.
- March *and* November: Weekends – 10:00 a.m. to 4:00 p.m.
- December, January and February: By Appointment

Garibaldi Maritime Museum
112 Garibaldi Ave.
Garibaldi, OR 97118
503-322-8411

☐ Historic U.S. Coast Guard Boathouse - Pier's End

Looking out over Tillamook Bay from Garibaldi, it's hard to miss the Historic U.S. Coast Guard Boathouse. Located at the end of a 760' pier, the longest on the Oregon Coast, it was built in 1936 to house two 36-foot motor lifeboats and a 26-foot oar-powered surfboat. Over the years, however, it was decommissioned and the neglected building, exposed to the coastal elements, fell into a state of disrepair. Today the boathouse is being restored and opened to the public as a heritage site dedicated to preserving the legacy of those who bravely served ships and sailors in distress off the Oregon Coast.

To access the pier, turn south onto 12th street from US Highway 101, and then turn right onto Bay Lane. Follow this to the parking area for the pier.

☐ Garibaldi Days

If it's the fourth weekend in July, then it's time for Garibaldi Days! Watch the fun Garibaldi Days Parade make its way through town, and then hop aboard the Oregon Coast Scenic Railway to ride a steam train up to Rockaway Beach and back before perusing locally made crafts and food items at over 60 different vendor booths. Then enjoy some live music, have your face painted, and settle in to watch a spectacular fireworks display over the bay. It's a great way to spend the day or the weekend!

TILLAMOOK, OR

Located on Tillamook Bay, the busy town of Tillamook is the "base" for the many adventures and destinations found in this portion of the coast. Plan on spending the day or a weekend to ride a steam train or pedal the rails, hike to a beautiful waterfall, tour a historic lighthouse, step back in time at a local museum, try your hand at catching some crabs, embark on the Three Capes Scenic Drive, or take in The Creamery, the single most visited destination in Oregon.

 ☐ **Oregon Coast Railriders**

A truly unique Oregon Coast adventure!

Sit down aboard a custom-built four-seater railrider and pedal 12 miles round-trip along an abandoned rail line from Bay City to Tillamook to experience the Oregon Coast like never before. Being a former rail line, the grade is only ½ percent, so it's an adventure the entire family can enjoy, as well as nature enthusiasts, cyclists, birders, and of course, rail fans.

Note: Plan on arriving 30 minutes before your departure to sign in, be assigned a railcar, and load. Most round-trips take approximately 2 hours and 45 minutes total. Departures occur at 9:00 a.m., 12:00 noon and 3:00 p.m.

- There are two guides with each trip
- $24 Per person 12 years and older
- $12 per child 11 years and younger when accompanied by an adult – Car seats can be accommodated – Let them know of your need for a seat when making a reservation
- Each guest must weigh 250 lbs or less
- Pets are not allowed
- Please dress for the weather – OC Railriders usually rolls, rain or shine
- Open Thursday through Monday – 8:00 a.m. to 5:00 p.m.
- Closed early October until May
- Reservations are required – Reserve online at www.OCRailriders.com

Oregon Coast Railriders
5400 Hayes Oyster Drive
Bay City, OR 97107
541-786-6165
Info@OCRailriders.com

☐ The Tillamook Creamery

No visit to Tillamook is complete without a visit to The Tillamook Creamery. A very popular Oregon icon, the factory itself and the Tillamook Cheese and Tillamook Ice Cream it produces are known statewide and around the world. Here, visitors take a self-guided tour through the newly remodeled state-of-the-art factory to see the entire cheese making process, from the arrival of fresh milk from the dairy farms surrounding

Tillamook to the production of curds and whey, and finally the different cheese products enjoyed by so many. Be sure to stop in and see this popular family friendly attraction while in Tillamook, have some breakfast, lunch or dinner, and don't forget to enjoy a tasty ice cream treat before you go!

The Tillamook Creamery
4175 US-101
Tillamook, OR 97141
503-815-1300

- Open Monday through Sunday – 8:00 a.m. to 6:00 p.m., 8:00 p.m. in the summer.

☐ Blue Heron French Cheese Company

Pull into the Blue Heron Cheese Company, walk past the vintage tractors and roaming roosters, step inside the 1930s era Dutch Colonial barn and you'll discover a Tillamook favorite offering an abundance of fine cheeses, Northwest wines, gift baskets, chocolate truffles and confections, coffees, teas, cocoas and more. In addition, grab a bite to eat at the deli, offering sandwiches with homemade soups and salads.

Blue Heron French Cheese Company
2001 Blue Heron Rd. Ste A
Tillamook, OR 97141
503-842-8281

- Open Monday through Sunday – 8:00 a.m. to 6:00 p.m.

www.Discover-Oregon.com

☐ Tillamook County Pioneer Museum

Located in the old courthouse building, the Tillamook County Pioneer Museum preserves the history of the Tillamook area, as well as the north coast, showcasing the early Native Americans of the region, explorers who arrived by ship and foot, pioneering families,  early industries and more. In addition, the museum features an impressive collection of the region's wildlife, as well as a special room dedicated to Abraham Lincoln, which includes a rare document signed by the President.

Note: If you're looking for an interesting book about the Oregon Coast, then be sure to check out the museum's large selection of local books in their museum store.

Tillamook County Pioneer Museum
2106 2nd Street
Tillamook, OR 97141
503-842-4553

- Open Tuesday through Sunday – 10:00 a.m. to 4:00 p.m.

☐ Tillamook Air Museum

 The first thing that strikes you about the building for the Tillamook Air Museum, a former WWII era blimp hangar, is its immense size. Step inside, look up, and be amazed at this massive wooden structure. You've never seen anything like it. Nearby, you'll

45

find perhaps a dozen or so rare and vintage aircraft parked within a large tent inside the hangar. Outside the tent, yet still inside the blimp hangar, is a collection of other vehicles, which changes from time to time and may include some vintage fire trucks, military vehicles, and even a steam engine being stored for the Oregon Coast Scenic Railroad.

Tillamook Air Museum
6030 Hangar Road
Tillamook, OR 97141
503-842-1130

- Open: Summer - Monday through Sunday – 10:00 a.m. to 5:00 p.m. – Closed on Mondays during the winter.

☐ Tillamook Farmers Market

At 40 booths in size, the Tillamook Farmers Market is one of the larger farmers markets on the Oregon coast. Here, you'll find a wide selection of items produced by local artisans, farmers, ranchers, fishermen, and even coffee growers. Stop at each booth to find handmade gifts and toys, jewelry, woodwork, pottery, plants, artwork and more, as well as baked items, tasty treats, and locally grown fruits and vegetables.

The Tillamook Farmers Market operates every Saturday from 9:00 a.m. to 2:00 p.m. at Laurel & 2nd Street in Tillamook during mid-June to the end of September.

☐ Munson Creek Falls State Park

Consisting of 62 acres of dense green and cool coastal forest, Munson Creek Falls State Park is home to towering Western Red Cedars, Big Leaf Maples, Red Alders and the second tallest Sitka Spruce in the world, measuring in at 260' in height! Yet as dramatic as that is, the main feature of the park is graceful Munson Falls. Comprised of three tiers, it falls 319' to the forest floor, making it the tallest waterfall in the coast range. Hike the popular and easy ¼ mile trail to the falls anytime of the year, and be sure to look for spawning salmon in Munson Creek during the late fall and winter months. Note that you cannot hike all the way to the falls, as the trail ends perhaps 50 yards from its base.

• The park is open daily from 8:00 a.m. to 8:00 p.m.

Munson Creek Falls State Park
Munson Creek Rd.
Tillamook, OR 97141

Directions: Look for the sign for *Munson Creek Natural Site* on Hwy 101 at 7.3 miles south of Tillamook. Turn east here onto Munson Creek Road and follow the well signed road to the state park. Note that the last segment of the road is one-lane with small pullouts, as well as some decent potholes. Driving this is not a problem in a passenger car, but we wouldn't advise hauling a camper trailer to the trailhead.

www.Discover-Oregon.com

Three Capes Scenic Loop, Pacific City, Neskowin, Otis, Lincoln City & Depoe Bay

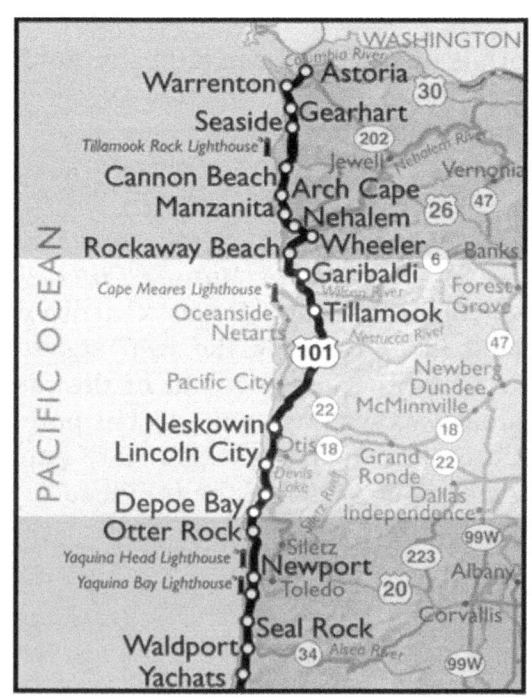

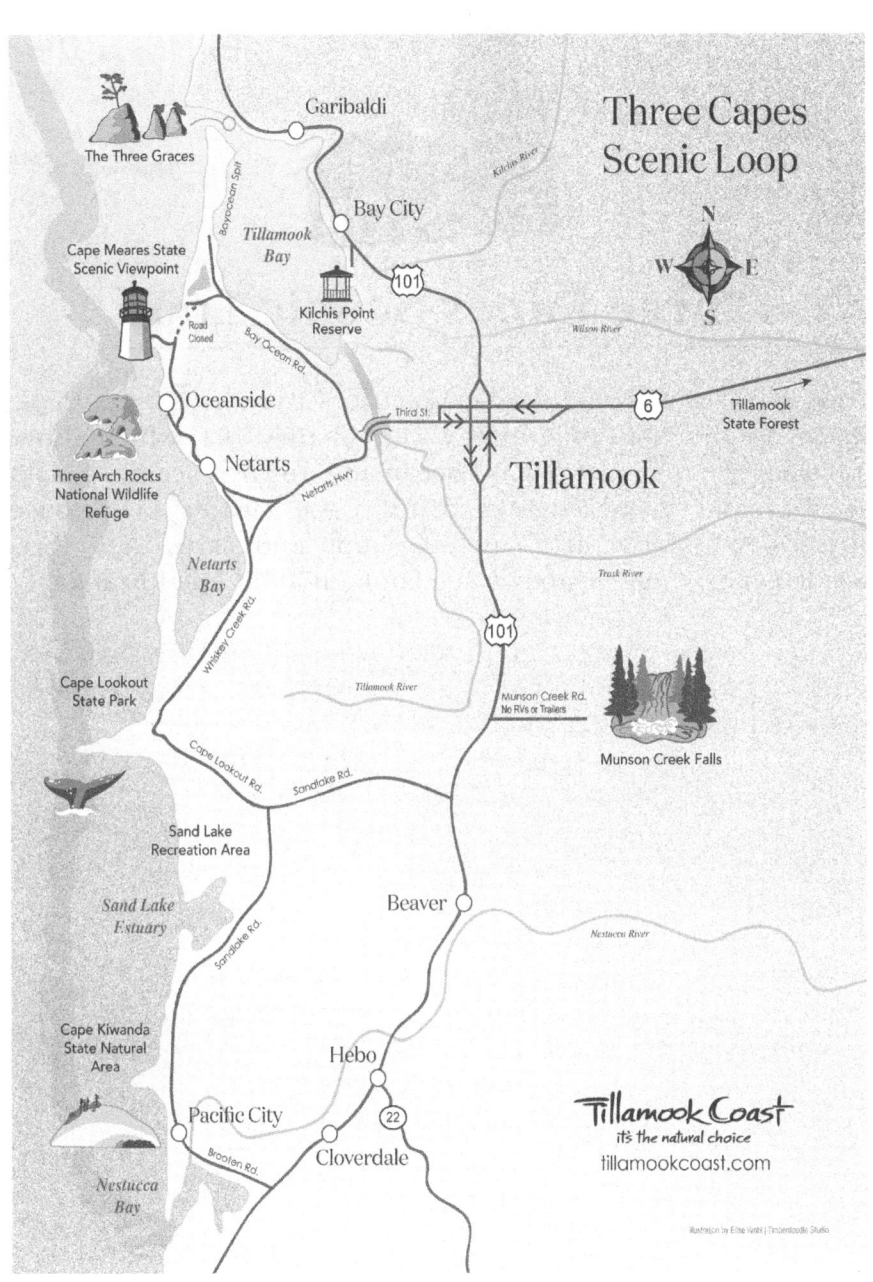

Map courtesy of www.TimberDoodleStudio.com

Three Capes Scenic Loop

Traveling from Tillamook to Pacific City, the Three Capes Scenic Loop is a 40 mile byway west of Hwy 101, which allows travelers to discover small oceanside towns, scenic coastal beaches and vistas, the beautiful Cape Meares Lighthouse, numerous historic sites, quaint shops and cafes, and three scenic capes; Cape Meares, Cape Lookout and Cape Kiwanda.

Driving Directions: Within "downtown" Tillamook, turn west onto 3rd Street, which will place you on 3rd Street / Highway 131 heading west. Follow this for 1.8 miles to Bayocean Road NW, which leads to Cape Meares. Turn right onto Bayocean Road NW to begin the Three Capes Scenic Loop.

Important: Note that as of summer 2018, Bayocean Road NW does not extend counterclockwise to the Cape Meares Lighthouse due to a road closure. As a result, you'll need to skip turning onto Bayocean Road NW and instead continue past it on Highway 131 south and approach Cape Meares in a clockwise manner from the south, via Netarts and then Oceanside. See the map on the previous page, and follow the signs on the highway for Cape Meares via this "detour."

 ☐ **Three Capes Stop:** Cape Meares State Park and the Cape Meares Lighthouse

Home to the shortest lighthouse in Oregon, commanding ocean views, and the largest flocks of Murres in the United States, the Cape Meares Scenic Viewpoint and lighthouse offers plenty for its visitors. From the parking lot, walk the 0.2 mile paved downhill path to the short walkway above the lighthouse. From here, take in the scenic vista over the Pacific Ocean before descending down to the lighthouse itself. Join a free lighthouse tour anytime between 11:00 a.m. and 4:00 p.m. to see up close the lighthouse's impressive Fresnel lens and to learn about the history of the cape and its historic beacon. Afterwards, take the short trail south, which winds its way atop a towering cliff face with an amazing view to the ocean below, and take a moment to sit on one of the benches placed along the way. (The first one offers a better view than the second

one.) Now return to the parking lot and cross it to find the 0.1 mile trail that leads to the interesting Octopus Tree and another beautiful view. Before you head back to your car, be sure to stop over at the viewing platform at the north end of the parking area for another impressive view.

Driving Directions: From the turn for Bayocean Road NW, continue northwest for 3.3 miles and turn left / south onto Bayshore Drive. Continue on Bayshore Drive for 2 miles to Cape Meares Lighthouse Drive. Turn right here and follow the signs to the parking for the lighthouse.

 **Three Capes Stop:** Oceanside, Oregon

South of Cape Meares is the small quaint town of Oceanside, Oregon. Located at the ocean's edge, it lives up to its name, offering travelers a beautiful beach to stroll upon while taking in views of the sea stacks of the Three Arch Rocks National Wildlife Refuge just off shore.

Driving Directions: Return to Bayshore Drive and proceed south for 2.5 miles to Oceanside, where the scenic loop connects with the Netarts Oceanside Hwy W.

 **Three Capes Stop:** Netarts, Oregon

A quick right turn off of the Three Capes Scenic Loop will drop you right into the small town of Netarts, Oregon, located at the mouth of the 7 mile long Netarts Bay.

Driving Directions: From Oceanside, proceed south on the Three Capes Scenic Loop / Netarts Oceanside Hwy W. for 2 miles to Netarts.

 **Three Capes Stop:** Nevør Shellfish Farm

Located on Netarts Bay is the Nevør Shellfish Farm. Open to the public, it sells fresh Torkes, Kumamotos and Olympia oysters that have been sustainably grown and harvested in Netarts Bay, a natural environment that is immersed with sea water twice a day, leading to some of the freshest and most delicious oysters you've ever tasted. Stop in to pick up a dozen or two.

- Open Monday through Saturday – 10:00 a.m. to 5:00 p.m.

Nevør Shellfish Farm
6060 Whiskey Creek Rd.
Netarts Bay, OR 97141
503-812-5071

Driving Directions: From Netarts, drive to the south end of town and turn right onto Netarts Bay Drive. Follow this for 1.4 miles to where it connects with Whiskey Creek Road. Proceed south on Whiskey Creek Road (Still the Three Capes Scenic Loop) for 1 mile to the Nevør Shellfish Farm on the right.

 ☐ **Three Capes Stop:** Jacobsen Salt Company

Make your way down the narrow gravel roadway and find the small Jacobsen Salt Company, manufacturer of America's finest hand-harvested sea salt, which is made right on the bank of Netarts Bay. Inside the small gift shop, you'll find the very  same gourmet salts they sell throughout Oregon and the world, including such flavors as Vanilla Bean, Lemon Zest, Pinot Noir, Smoked Cherrywood, Ghost Chili, Black Garlic and more. And yes, they're all salts! In addition, you'll find tasty confections, such as chocolates, black licorice, caramels and honey nut chews. You'll want to buy a gift pack for yourself and your favorite chef. Be sure to see the tiny salt crystals they have on display.

Jacobsen Salt Company
9820 Whiskey Creek Road
Tillamook, OR 97141
503-719-4973

- Open: Monday through Sunday – 10:00 a.m. to 5:00 p.m., December through February – 10:00 a.m. to 4:00 p.m.

Driving Directions: From the Nevør Shellfish Farm, continue south on Whiskey Creek Road for 1.8 miles to the Jacobsen Salt Company on the right. Proceed down the narrow driveway to the parking area.

 ☐ **Three Capes Stop:** Cape Lookout State Park

Jutting out into the ocean like a long straight-edged dagger, Cape Lookout is a cape like no other on the Oregon coast. Here, you'll find towering cliff faces rising more than 800' high along its two-mile length and offering dramatic views of the ocean below. And because visitors are above the ocean instead of standing at sea level next to it, Cape Lookout is an excellent whale watching location, as it provides the unique perspective of looking down upon the whales from above, instead out from the shoreline.

The cape also offers a few adventurous hikes. To see the captivating view at the tip of the cape, hike the Cape Trail.

Cape Trail – An easy to moderately difficult trail with interesting trees and numerous scenic viewpoints leads from the parking lot to the viewpoint at the tip of the cape. 2.4 Miles one way with 400' of elevation gain. Note that sections of the trail can be very muddy in wet weather, so wear appropriate footwear. Note, as well, that the tip of the cape, as well as numerous viewpoints along the trail, sit atop cliffs rising over 800' above the ocean, so be mindful of small children and pets.

Driving Directions: From the Jacobsen Salt Company, continue south on the Three Capes Scenic Loop for 3.7 miles to the parking for the Cape Lookout Trailhead on your right. Note that there are a couple of viewpoints of the cape along your drive, one of which is at the west end of the Cape Lookout State Park Campground, which you will pass at the 1.0 mile mark.

PACIFIC CITY

 ☐ **Three Capes Stop:** Pacific City and Cape Kiwanda State Park

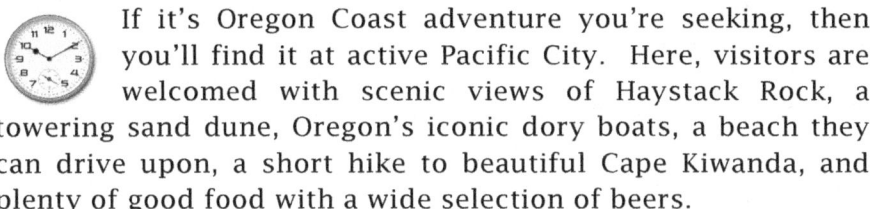 If it's Oregon Coast adventure you're seeking, then you'll find it at active Pacific City. Here, visitors are welcomed with scenic views of Haystack Rock, a towering sand dune, Oregon's iconic dory boats, a beach they can drive upon, a short hike to beautiful Cape Kiwanda, and plenty of good food with a wide selection of beers.

Haystack Rock

Perhaps the first thing you notice when you pull into Pacific City from the north is impressive Haystack Rock, one of two towering sea stacks in the state sharing this name. Park for free in the large public parking lot opposite the Pelican Brewing Company, or  drive down the large concrete ramp to park on the beach itself, which is an interesting experience. Note: Make sure the sand is not currently piled at the base of the ramp, as cars and trucks do get stuck here in the soft dry sand. Take note of the conditions at the base of the ramp, as well as the number of cars that have successfully driven and parked on the beach before making your way down. Park to the *south* of the ramp, as the area to the north is reserved for Dory fishermen.

Explore Cape Kiwanda

Now make your way towards the large sand dune that dominates the landscape to the north and hike the obvious trail making its way up and left towards the ocean. Once atop the plateau, you'll discover multiple overlooks offering views of yellow, orange and rust colored sandstone cliffs carved into dramatic seascapes by the relentless ocean waves. Folks in the know make it a point to visit the cape during periods of heavy surf to watch spectacular displays of large waves exploding as they crash against the cliffs.   *Cape Kiwanda photo © Shane Kucera*

The Large Sand Dune

What's a trip to the Oregon Coast without gaining a summit? Return to the large sand dune and make your way to the top at 230' high. Your reward?...a speedy descent! Join your fellow sand hill enthusiasts and run full speed downhill to the base, filling your shoes with sand and your day with fun memories!

The Dory Fleet

If you're lucky, you'll spot some dory boats from Oregon's iconic Dory Fleet both launching and coming ashore near the base of the giant sand hill. These small high-sided yet shallow draft boats with high bows actually launch and land in the surf. If you see any dory boats in the vicinity, be sure to hang around and watch this Oregon Coast fishing tradition that reaches back over 115 years. *Photo courtesy of PacificCityFishing.com*

Pelican Brewing Company

You've had a busy afternoon, so head over to the Pelican Brewing Company near the parking area and enjoy some great food and a wide selection of excellent Oregon beers.

Dory Days

During mid-July of each year, Pacific City hosts Dory Days, a celebration of Oregon's unique Dory Boat fishing tradition, as well as the Oregon Coast lifestyle. Sponsored by the Pacific City-Nestucca Valley Chamber of Commerce and the Pacific City Dorymen's Association, visitors are welcome to enjoy a fun and colorful parade featuring decorated Dory Boats, live music, an artisan fair featuring local goods and crafts, kids activities, a hearty pancake breakfast and more.

Driving Directions: To reach the parking for Haystack Rock, Cape Kiwanda and the Pelican Brewing Company, continue south on Cape Lookout Road from the Cape Lookout Trailhead for 3.3 miles to Sandlake Road. Turn right / south here and continue on Sandlake Road for 6.4 miles to where it continues onto McPhillips Drive. Stay on McPhillips Drive for another 1.4 miles to the large parking area for the beach on your right.

The Grateful Bread Bakery

Step inside to find this small local bakery humming with activity. Enjoy breakfast, lunch, or dinner, as well as some of their freshly made breads and baked goods. Another one of our favorite places on the coast!

Grateful Bread Bakery
34805 Brooten Rd.
Cloverdale, OR 97112
503-965-7337

- Open: Thurs. through Mon. – 8:00 a.m. to 9:00 p.m. – Winter hours are 8:00 a.m. to 8:00 p.m. Closed mid-day.

NESKOWIN, OR

Neskowin is a small beach town with a friendly neighborhood feel. Better yet, it offers a *long* beautiful stretch of beach, perfect for walking, which is anchored at its southern end by Proposal Rock. Park your car at the parking area just off Hwy 101 and take the obvious path south of the lot, next to the creek, or walk west through the neighborhood streets to admire the quaint cottages and homes before reaching the beach. If you're here during the 4th of July, then be sure to enjoy the whimsical patriotic parade in the morning.

☐ **Cascade Head Preserve Hike & Viewpoint**

The easy, short, and mostly level Nature Conservancy Trail takes hikers 1 mile through a beautiful coastal forest before reaching a grassy bluff offering one of the Oregon Coast's most iconic views, with the Pacific Ocean and the Salmon River Estuary far below. Keep an eye out for deer, elk, wildflowers, birds and butterflies.

Driving Directions: At a point 3.5 miles south of Neskowin, turn west off of Hwy 101 at the turnoff for the Cascade Head Preserve. Note that this turnoff is right at a crest in the road. Follow this well-maintained gravel road for 3.1 miles to the Nature Conservancy Trailhead. If you'd like to do some more hiking, you'll find the trailhead for the 2.7 mile Hart's Cove trail 1 mile further down the road.

OTIS, OR

☐ Drift Creek Covered Bridge

Oregon is home to a wealth of covered bridges, 54 of them, in fact! Built in 1914, the Drift Creek Covered Bridge has quite a history. Destroyed by a flood in 1933, the bridge was rebuilt, but over time fell into a state of disrepair, eventually being scheduled by the State for demolition in 1997. However, local residents Kerry and Laura Sweitz offered to move the bridge to their property eight miles away, where they just happened to have a concrete bridge with the exact same dimensions. Through a lot of hard work on their part and other volunteers over the course of four years, the bridge was completely dismantled and then reassembled on the Sweitz's property, where it resides today.

Drift Creek Covered Bridge
1111 Bear Creek Road
Lincoln City, OR 97367

Note that as you drive to and from the Drift Creek Covered Bridge from Hwy 101, you'll pass the small **Otis Café** on the north side of Hwy 18. If you're hungry, then this is an excellent place to grab a bite to eat.

LINCOLN CITY, OR

One of the most popular destinations on Oregon's "mid-coast", Lincoln City bustles with activity on any summer day. In addition to countless shops, a casino, a factory outlet mall and much more, Lincoln City is home to a seven mile long beach which hosts a myriad activities, including the popular Lincoln City Summer Kite Festival in June, the Fall Kite Festival in October, countless beach picnics, and an army of Float Fairies, who, as part of Lincoln City's "Finders Keepers" promotion, hide over 2,000 colorful glass floats between mid-October and Memorial Day each year anywhere along the seven mile shore, between the high tide line and the embankment. Since it's "finders keepers", if you find one, it's yours to keep! *Photo © Cody Cha*

☐ Roads End State Recreation Site

Located at the northern end of town is Roads End State Recreation Site. A short trail from the large paved parking lot leads to a long stretch of beach, which is usually not as busy as others in Lincoln City. Stroll north from the parking lot to scenic Roads End Point and keep an eye out for colorful glass floats along the way. Every year, between mid-October to Memorial Day, thousands of glass floats, as well as sea stars, sand dollars and other creatures, are hidden along Lincoln City beaches by "Float Fairies", and Roads End is a popular place to find them. Of course, if you find one, then it's yours to keep.

☐ D River Beach Wayside

The D River, known in these parts as the "shortest river in the world", leads directly to one of the busiest beaches on the Oregon Coast. With easy access off of Highway 101 and a large paved parking area next to the beach, it bustles  with activity for much of the year, especially during each June and October, when it hosts the world's largest kite festivals. Check online to see this year's kite festival schedule that makes Lincoln City the "Kite Capital of the World."

Photo © Lincoln City Visitor & Convention Bureau

☐ Lincoln City Farmers & Crafters Market

Featuring an abundance of locally made and grown goods, including cheeses, honey, coffee, meats, baked goods, nursery plants, tasty foods and sweet treats, hand-crafted items, fresh seasonal produce and more.

Lincoln City Farmers & Crafters Market
At the Lincoln City Cultural Center
540 NE Hwy 101
Lincoln City, OR 97365

- Open Sunday – 9:00 a.m. to 3:00 p.m. – Early May to mid-October

North Lincoln County Historical Museum

This small yet highly regarded museum conveys the history of Lincoln City and the surrounding area. Stop in during a summer's day or a rainy December weekend and admire the impressive collection of displays showcasing Native American artifacts, glass floats from Japan, antique toys, 1950s advertising, the important industries of the area, and more. Admission is free.

North Lincoln County Historical Museum
4907 US Highway 101
Lincoln City, OR 97367
541-996-6614

* Open:

    Summer: June through August – Wednesday through Sunday – 12:00 p.m. to 5:00 p.m.

    Winter: September through December 15th and February through May 31st – Wednesday through Saturday – 12:00 p.m. to 5:00 p.m.

Nelscott House Antiques

If you're a fan of Disneyana collectibles, then you'll like the Nelscott House Antiques shop. Stop in to see their amazing collection for sale, and be sure to ask about their rare "uranium glass" items from the 1930s. They glow in the dark!

Nelscott House Antiques
3200 US-101
Lincoln City, OR 97367
541-994-9761

- Open Monday through Saturday – 9:00 a.m. to 5:00 p.m., Sunday 10:00 a.m. to 5:00 p.m.

DEPOE BAY, OR

☐ Boiler Bay State Scenic Viewpoint

In 1910, the ocean freighter J. Marhoffer was making its way to Portland when it caught fire after a crewman attempted to light a gas lamp. All hands on board abandoned ship before the vessel ran ashore and exploded, sending debris flying for half a mile into the air. Today, all that remains of the ship is its boiler, which can be seen amongst the rocks during low tides.

Boiler Bay is an excellent location at which to spot gray whales year-round, as well as an abundance of ocean-going birds. Park in the large paved lot and take a path out along the fence line to the viewpoint. Located 1 mile north of Depoe Bay.

Boiler Bay State Wayside
Depoe Bay, 97341

☐ Depoe Bay Whale Watching Center

 Located inside a building on the seawall overlooking the ocean in Depoe Bay, the Whale Watching Center is staffed with Oregon State Park personnel who are happy to answer your questions and help you spot some of the nearly 20,000 Gray Whales that migrate past the center each year on their way between Alaska and Mexico. Beginning with a surge in March and continuing through June, the Spring migration brings an abundance of whales making their way north to Alaska, while Summer and Fall bring fewer migrating whales, but a pod of about 20 make their summer home just off Depoe Bay, where visitors can easily spot them spouting, spyhopping and diving.

Depoe Bay Whale Watching Center
119 US-101
Depoe Bay, OR 97341
541-765-3304

- Open: Monday through Sunday – 10:00 a.m. to 4:00 p.m. Closed Mondays and Tuesdays during the winter.

www.Discover-Oregon.com

 **Carrie's Whale Watching Tours & Whale, Sealife and Shark Museum**

It's one thing to see glimpses of the majestic whales from land, but it is a dramatically different experience to see them from the water. Join Carrie Newell, a Marine Biologist with a PhD in Marine Biology, and her captains aboard a Zodiac for a 1.5 hour educational excursion on the ocean just off Depoe Bay. Here, you'll learn all about the many fascinating sea animals that inhabit Oregon's coastal waters, including the approximately 20 resident Gray Whales, which spend their summer just offshore.

- Rates: $40 per person. Children 12 and under are $32. Children under 2 years of age are not allowed. Each trip is 1.5 hours, though 1 and 2 hour trips are also available. Inquire about these when booking your trip.

- Book your trip at 541-912-6734 or online (Recommended) at www.OregonWhales.com. Reservations for whale watching trips should be made 3 to 5 days in advance during the summer months. Call *the morning before* your departure to check weather conditions for the day of your trip. Check in at the museum ½ hour prior to your departure time.

- Departures are at 10:00 a.m., 12:00 p.m. and 2:00 p.m.

- Daily trips are scheduled according to the current ocean conditions, and your excursion will not go out in rough seas. There is little chance of getting sea sickness, and travelers seldom get wet. Note that temperatures on the ocean can be chilly, so dress accordingly. It's best to have jackets, hats and gloves available.

Carrie's Whale Watching Tours
234 US-101
Depoe Bay, OR 97341
541-912-6734

- Open Monday through Sunday – 10:00 a.m. to 4:00 p.m. – Winter Hours: 11:00 a.m. to 4:00 p.m.

Otter Crest Loop, Yaquina Bay Recreation Site, Nye Beach, Newport & Toledo

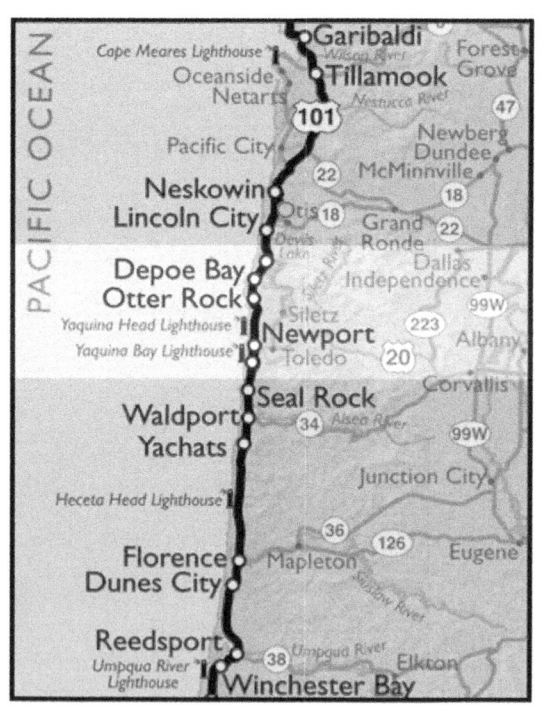

OTTER CREST LOOP

As with the Three Capes Scenic Loop, the Charleston to Bandon Scenic Tour Route, and the Cape Arago Beach Loop, the 3.6 mile Otter Crest Loop steers travelers off of Hwy 101 for a slower paced journey along a more scenic section of the coast. Here, those who decide to explore will be rewarded with panoramic vistas, scenic viewpoints, intriguing coastal features and even a spouting whale or two!

Note that a 1.2 mile portion of the Otter Crest Loop narrows down to a one-way road southbound, so you'll want to start at the northern end of the loop and make one continuous drive until you reach Hwy 101 again at its southern terminus.

You'll find the northern entrance to the Otter Crest Loop at approximately 2 miles south of Depoe Bay. (2.2 Miles from the bridge over Depoe Bay) Look for a small sign on your right that reads *Otter Crest Lp.* and veer off to your right here. Reset your odometer at this point. The road will reduce down to one lane for 1.2 miles at the 0.7 mile mark.

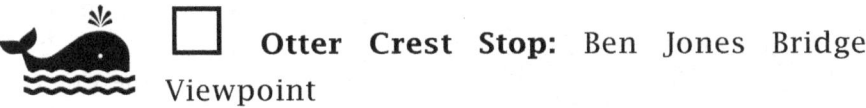 **Otter Crest Stop:** Ben Jones Bridge Viewpoint

Designed by Conde McCullough, who was the primary engineer of the many graceful bridges spanning the Oregon Coast Highway, the Ben Jones Bridge seen here is a tribute to the "Father of the Oregon Coast Highway", Ben Jones, the man who introduced legislation for the funding and construction of the highway in 1919.

At 0.3 miles after entering the Otter Crest Loop, look for a large paved pullout and viewing area on the right immediately after crossing the bridge.

 ☐ Otter Crest Stop: Cape Foulweather and Otter Crest State Scenic Viewpoint

Chances are both the weather and the view will be stunning when you stop by the Otter Crest State Scenic Viewpoint during your drive. However, back in March of 1778, the seas were rough, the winds fierce, and the skies were foul when Captain Cook first laid eyes on Oregon and named the cape just to the north for the conditions he and his crew were enduring that day, Cape Foulweather. You, on the other hand, can stand on a point 500' above the ocean and enjoy sunny skies, panoramic vistas, and if you keep an eye out, a passing Gray Whale!

At 1.8 miles, park in the large paved lot at the Otter Crest State Scenic Viewpoint and walk a short distance to the viewpoint, as well as the nearby Lookout Observatory and Gift Shop.

 ☐ Otter Crest Stop: Devil's Punchbowl State Natural Area

Located in the small beach community of Otter Rock, OR, the Devil's Punchbowl is a unique Oregon Coast geologic feature. Here, a massive bowl in the rock with openings to the ocean fills with water during high tide and stormy seas to create a churning "punchbowl" of waves and foam. Travelers can walk within it during low tide, and the area is an excellent location for spotting whales.

Note: This area is also a favorite spot for surfers.

At 3.2 miles, turn right / west onto 1st Street and continue 0.4 miles to the parking area for Devil's Punchbowl.

 **Otter Crest Stop:** Flying Dutchman Winery

Located adjacent to the Devil's Punchbowl State Natural Area, the Flying Dutchman Winery is the only working winery on the Oregon Coast. Stop in to enjoy their award-winning wines in a wind-sheltered grove of shore pines offering a memorable ocean view. A gift shop offering just the right souvenir or wine-related gift is also available.

Flying Dutchman Winery
915 First Street
Otter Rock, OR 97369
541-765-2553

Located at the Devil's Punchbowl parking area.

 **Otter Crest Stop:** Mo's Seafood & Chowder

An Oregon Coast favorite since 1946, Mo's chowder is the perfect lunch or dinnertime treat, and it seems the more inclement the weather, the better the chowder! Stop in at the small Mo's Seafood & Chowder next to the Flying Dutchman Winery for a classic taste of the Oregon Coast!

Mo's Seafood & Chowder
122 First Street
Otter Rock, OR 97369
541-765-2442

Located at the Devil's Punchbowl parking area.

NEWPORT, OR

Located mid-coast, Newport is a larger coastal town that offers a wealth of diverse activities. Walk beautiful Beverly Beach, step back in time at Oregon's tallest lighthouse, spot passing Gray Whales, visit a bustling bayfront, see the state's finest aquarium, charter a fishing boat, walk a jetty out into the ocean, and the list goes on and on. You can easily spend a day or two or three here, so make your plans to head to Newport!

☐ **Beverly Beach State Park**

If you're looking for a long sandy beach to walk and explore, then you'll find it at Beverly Beach State Park, just north of Newport. Here the shoreline stretches from Yaquina Head and its picture perfect lighthouse to the south all the way to the headlands of Otter Rock reaching into the waves to the north. While walking the beach, keep an eye out for surfers, and take some time to look for fossilized sea shells in the cliff faces.

 ☐ **Yaquina Head Outstanding Natural Area**

Standing majestically at the end of a mile long cape is the historic Yaquina Head Lighthouse. Oregon's tallest lighthouse at 93', this unwavering beacon has guided ships ashore and to safety for nearly 150 years. Today, travelers can take guided tours of the lighthouse, enjoy spotting whales as they migrate past the viewpoint, explore the nearby tide pools to find sea stars, crabs, sea anemones and more, and visit the nearby large interpretive center to learn all about the history of the lighthouse and shipping off the Oregon coast.

45 Minute guided tours occur up to 12 times per day during the summer, and reservations are strongly recommended during the busy summer months. Winter tours occur more sporadically. Tickets are available on a first-come, first-served basis at the Interpretive Center on the day of your visit. Reservations may be made up to 90 days in advance during July through September by calling 1-877-444-6777 or visiting www.Recreation.gov. Note that space on the tours is limited.

The grounds open at 8:00 a.m. and close at sunset. There is a $7.00 per car entrance fee to the Natural Area.

By the way, Yaquina is pronounced "Yah Kwin Ah".

Yaquina Head Lighthouse & Interpretive Center
750 NW Lighthouse Drive
Newport, OR 97
541-574-3100

* Open: Monday through Friday – 10:00 a.m. to 4:00 p.m.

☐ Historic Nye Beach

At the northern edge of Newport, just a few blocks off of Highway 101, is the small neighborhood of Nye Beach. Officially 12 blocks long and 2 blocks deep, it is filled with 40 locally owned businesses, including shops of all kinds, restaurants, hotels, public  parking, beach access and more. It's a perfect area to walk about, explore and have some lunch. Note: Stroll to the beach, where you'll find a nice view of the Yaquina Head Lighthouse.

☐ Sylvia Beach Hotel

While strolling about Nye Beach, make your way over to the 1912 Sylvia Beach Hotel on NW Cliff Street, at the end of 3rd Street, and step inside to get a sense of this great place to stay while at the coast. Named after Sylvia Beach, the expatriate American bookseller and publisher who opened the small Shakespeare and Company bookstore in Paris, France, each of its 21 rooms are themed after a famous author, including Hemingway, F. Scott Fitzgerald, Mark Twain, J. K. Rowling and even Dr. Seuss. According to the hotel... *There are no telephones, TVs, or Wi-Fi in rooms at the Sylvia Beach Hotel. The allure is beach quiet. Unplug, unwind, and sleep with your favorite author.*

Sylvia Beach Hotel B & B
267 NW Cliff Street
Newport, OR 97365
541-265-5428

☐ The Olde Telephone Company

Step through the front door of the Olde Telephone Company and find hundreds of museum-quality antique phones, phone booths, signs, switchboards, and other phone-related paraphernalia on display. Then discover that everything you see is for sale! It's definitely unique and one of the most interesting "museums" on the coast.

The Olde Telephone Company
255 SW 9th Street
Newport, OR 97365
541-272-5225

- Open: Monday through Sunday – 10:00 a.m. to 5:00 p.m.

Yaquina Bay Lighthouse

While the Yaquina Head Lighthouse stands as a tall sentinel at the northern end of Newport, the older Yaquina Bay Lighthouse resides in a small house at the south end of town and guides ships to a long jetty, which leads them to Yaquina Bay.

Built atop a bluff at the mouth of the Yaquina River in 1871 and decommissioned only a few years later, in 1874, the Yaquina Bay Lighthouse is believed to be the oldest structure in Newport, and is the only historic wooden lighthouse still standing in Oregon.

Tour the lighthouse and its attached living quarters to see different rooms furnished just as they were in 1871, and make a point to go down to the basement where you can watch a short but interesting video about the lighthouse and its history. Tours are free, but donations are appreciated.

Yaquina Bay Lighthouse & State Recreation Site
Newport, OR 97365
541-265-5679

Lighthouse Hours:

- Monday through Friday – 10:00 a.m. to 4:00 p.m. - Memorial Day Weekend through the end of September.

- Monday through Friday – 12:00 p.m. to 4:00 p.m. – October to Memorial Day Weekend

☐ Newport's Historic Bayfront

Walk along Newport's bustling bayfront and you'll see a collection of retail shops, restaurants, chowder houses, and other tourist attractions, but don't think for a moment that it's not a working commercial bayfront first and foremost. Home to Oregon's largest commercial fishing fleet and a corresponding collection of large seafood processing plants, you'll see forklifts hoisting large pallets of fish on ice next to the small shop selling t-shirts extolling Oregon's coastal life. A bit rough and unkept around the edges, just as it should be, the bayfront offers a wide collection of sites, sounds and smells. Stop and have some lunch at Mo's, walk the docks to see trawlers returning with their catch, mosey over to the loud barking sea lions making a commotion, or rent a crab ring and toss it over a dock railing to try your hand at tricking a large Dungeness crab into taking the bait.

Park your car along the main boulevard or find a public parking spot and walk the bayfront.

Newport Historic Bayfront
250 – 300 SW Bay Blvd.
Newport, OR 97365

☐ Marine Discovery Tours

Give up your role of landlubber and hop aboard Marine Discovery Tours' 65' Discovery cruise vessel for a two-hour educational tour. Narrated by friendly naturalist guides, this hands-on tour searches for...and usually finds...gray whales, harbor seals, porpoises, sea lions, bald eagles, pelicans and more. In addition, you'll get to touch a variety of sea life, including Dungeness and Rock crab, sea stars, and whatever else is brought up out of the ocean depths.

The tour makes its way out onto the ocean, where you'll see the Oregon coastline from an all new perspective, as well as two lighthouses, Newport's impressive jetty, and Oregon's largest commercial fishing fleet within Yaquina Bay. If ocean conditions are rough, then the heated Discovery will explore the 6 miles of Yaquina Bay and the Yaquina River.

Sea Life and Whale Watching tours operate daily from March through October. *Photo © Marine Discovery Cruise*

Marine Discovery Cruise
345 SW Bay Blvd.
Newport, OR 97365
541-265-6200

- Summer Hours: Monday through Sunday – 10:00 a.m. to 6:00 p.m. Opening and closing hours can vary each day.

- Winter Hours: Monday through Sunday – 10:00 a.m. to 5:00 p.m.

 Ripley's Believe It or Not!

Long a staple of Newport Bay's waterfront, Ripley's Believe It or Not Museum is a light-hearted journey into the bizarre. Step inside to see a collection of oddities unlike anything you've ever seen before, including a towering Bigfoot, Liu Ch'ung, the man with a double set of pupils, an antique vampire killing kit, a portrait of Michael Jackson made with nail polish, and a half-man half-fish. The kids, of course, will love it.

Admission:

Adult: (13 and Older)	$14.99
Youth: (5 - 12)	$7.99
Child: (4 and Under)	Free

Ripley's Believe It or Not
250 SW Bay Blvd.
Newport, OR 97365
541-265-2206

- Open Monday through Friday – 11:00 a.m. to 5:00 p.m., Saturday and Sunday – 10:00 a.m. to 5:00 p.m.

The Wax Works

Aligned with Ripley's Believe It or Not! and the Oregon Undersea Gardens, The Wax Works takes visitors on a walking tour of over 100 full-sized wax figures depicting celebrities, movie stars and fictional characters, including Johnny Depp, Marilyn Monroe, Arnold Schwarzenegger, Spock, Michael Jackson, and major characters from Lord of the Rings, Star Wars, and Pirates of the Caribbean.

The Wax Works
250 SW Bay Blvd.
Newport, OR 97365
541-265-2206

- Open Monday through Friday – 11:00 a.m. to 5:00 p.m., Saturday and Sunday – 10:00 a.m. to 5:00 p.m.

Admission: Inquire about discounted admission pricing involving Ripley's Believe It or Not! and the Oregon Undersea Gardens.

☐ Oregon Undersea Gardens

Part of Mariner Square, along with Ripley's Believe It or Not! and The Wax Works, Oregon Undersea Gardens allows visitors to "descend beneath the sea" to experience a world filled with fish, anemones, crabs, a Giant Pacific Octopus, and more. Inquire as to when the next fish feeding occurs, and watch a SCUBA diver feed the fish.

Oregon Undersea Gardens
250 SW Bay Blvd.
Newport, OR 97365
541-265-2206

- Open Monday through Friday – 11:00 a.m. to 5:00 p.m., Saturday and Sunday – 10:00 a.m. to 5:00 p.m.

Admission: Inquire about discounted admission pricing involving Ripley's Believe It or Not! and The Wax Works.

 ☐ Oregon Coast Aquarium

Offering a world-class facility along Yaquina Bay, across from the historic waterfront, the Oregon Coast Aquarium is one of Oregon's top tourist attractions. Here, visitors can wander 23 acres to discover playful Sea Otters, an inquisitive Giant Pacific Octopus, colorful ocean birds, mesmerizing Jelly Fish, acrobatic Harbor Seals and Sea Lions, and much more, all as part of a marine educational attraction.

Plan on visiting for 1.5 to 2 hours. Free car and RV parking is available, and you'll also find the Ferry Slip Café, a coffee bar and a large gift shop. One third of the exhibits are outdoors, so dress accordingly. Pets are not allowed past the front gates.

Oregon Coast Aquarium
2820 SE Ferry Slip Road
Newport, OR 97365
541-867-3474

- Open Monday through Sunday – 10:00 a.m. to 5:00 p.m.

Admission:

Adult: (18 – 64)	$22.95
Senior: (65 +)	$19.95
Young Adult: (13 – 17)	$19.95
Child: (3 – 12)	$14.95

☐ Hatfield Marine Science Center

A working research lab, the Hatfield Marine Science Center studies and shares information on tsunamis, coastal erosion, sustainable fisheries, aquatic ecosystems and much more. In addition to its research, it operates an interpretive center, which is open to the public. Here, you can learn about the ocean environment through interesting displays and experience Tidepool Touch Tanks, where you can touch sea stars, sea urchins, abalone, anemones and other creatures found in the nearby coastal waters. If your timing is right, you may even be greeted by a Giant Pacific Octopus as you enter the exhibit area!

Admission is free, but a suggested donation of $5 per person or $20 per family is appreciated

Hatfield Marine Science Center
2030 SE Marine Science Drive
Newport, OR 97365
541-867-0100

- Summer Hours: Monday through Sunday - 10:00 a.m. to 5:00 p.m. - Memorial Day to Labor Day

- Winter Hours: Thursday through Monday - 10:00 a.m. to 4:00 p.m. - Labor Day to Memorial Day

☐ South Beach State Park – South Jetty

At the mouth of Yaquina Bay are two prominent jetties; North Jetty and South Jetty. To the immediate south of the South Jetty is South Beach State Park, which is an excellent beach for walking, horseback riding, fishing, clamming, and surfing. In addition, this beach is very popular with kiteboarders, who navigate the waves at high speeds with their colorful kites. Drive west on Southwest Jetty Way to where it terminates at the parking area and walk out on the beach to catch all the action.

Note: If you're looking for a little fishing adventure, stop in at a bait shop on the historic bayfront in Newport, pick up some sand shrimp, and head out onto the South Jetty with a sturdy fishing pole in hand to try your luck. With some patience, you just may land a large Starry Flounder, Ling Cod, or Cabezon. A fishing license is required, and since the rocky conditions here tend to eat tackle, you may want to use inexpensive weights, such as large washers. Remember, don't go out on the jetty if conditions are poor, and *never* turn your back on the ocean.

www.Discover-Oregon.com

☐ Ocean Coast Glassworks

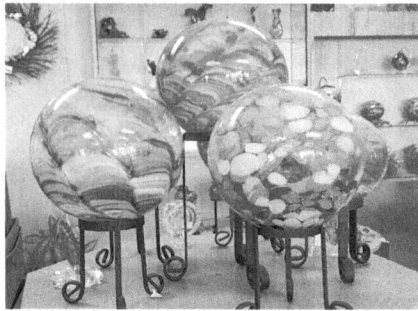 Located six blocks east of Hwy 101, Ocean Coast Glassworks offers visitors an opportunity to jump right in and handcraft their own beautiful glass float. Or if you prefer, simply take a seat and watch a glassblowing demonstration as the artisans create sea life sculptures, colorful shells, bowls, jewelry, paperweights and more, all from glass! Their gallery offers a very nice collection of hand blown works of art for sale, and you may also arrange a class by calling 541-574-8226.

Ocean Coast Glassworks
616 E Olive Street
Newport, OR 97365
541-574-8226

- Open Thursday through Tuesday – 11:00 a.m. to 5:00 p.m. – Closed Wednesday.

☐ Newport Farmers Market

 Rain or shine, the Newport Farmers Market welcomes visitors to experience a taste of Newport. Stop in and shop over 60 vendors for locally grown produce, honey, dairy products, fresh pastries, coffee, artwork, photography, nursery plants and more, all while striking up conversations with local farmers, Master Gardeners, and skilled artisans of the coast.

- Open:

  Summer and Fall: Saturdays – May through October – 9:00 a.m. to 1:00 p.m. - Located on the corner of Angle and Hwy 101.

  Winter and Spring: Saturdays – November though April – 9:00 a.m. to 1:00 p.m. – Located at the Lincoln County Fairgrounds Exhibit Hall, 633 NE 3rd Street, Newport, OR.

☐ Yaquina Pacific Railroad Historical Society

If you know the difference between a 2-8-2 and a 4-4-0, then you'll want to visit the Yaquina Pacific Railroad Historical Society Museum. Located 7 miles east of Newport in the town of Toledo, this small museum run by dedicated volunteers showcases a 1922 Baldwin steam locomotive, a 1951 switching locomotive, the oldest restored wooden caboose in the Pacific Northwest, and an intricately restored Railway Post Office and baggage car. Though you can walk around the collection if the museum is closed, you'll want to stop in when it is open so the docents can explain the history of the locomotives and rolling stock, as well as the important role they played in shaping the history of Lincoln County. Admission is free, though donations are accepted. *Photo courtesy of Martin E. Hansen.*

Yaquina Pacific Railroad Historical Society
100 NW A Street
Toledo, OR 97391
541-336-5256

- Open Tuesday through Saturday – 10:00 a.m. to 2:00 p.m. – Closed Sunday and Monday.

 Toledo History Center

Located 7 miles inland from Newport, via Hwy 20, is the small town of Toledo, Oregon. Settled in 1866, its rich history reflects the industries that flourished in the forests of the Coast Range to the east and the mighty Pacific Ocean to the west. Stop in at the small Toledo History Center to see an interesting collection of exhibits that explain the history of Toledo and the different roles that timber, boat building, dairy farming and the railroad played in shaping the town through the years.

Toledo History Center
208 South Main Street
Toledo, OR 97391
541-336-1203

- Open: Wednesday through Sunday – 12:00 p.m. to 4:00 p.m.

Note: Also be sure to also stop by and visit the Toledo Waterfront Market at Waterfront Park. Here, you'll find locally made arts and crafts, clothing, fresh produce, fruit, food, and more. The market operates every Thursday from 10:00 a.m. to 3:00 p.m., June through September.

Seal Rock, Waldport, Yachats, Cape Perpetua & Heceta Head

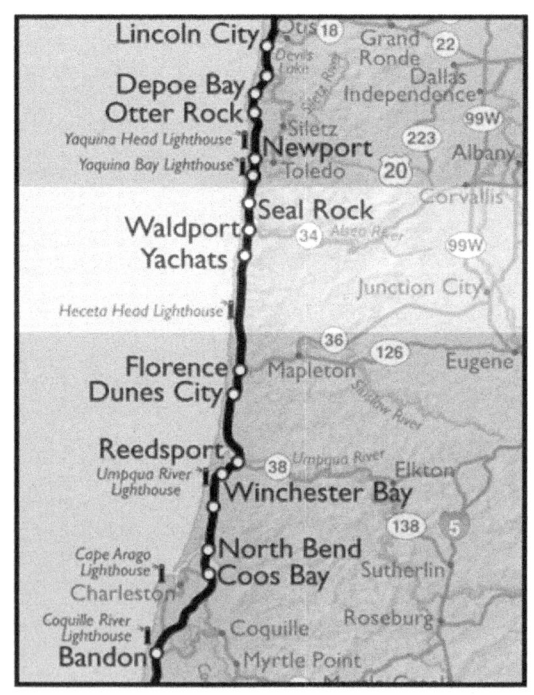

Seal Rock, Or

☐ Ocean Beaches Glassblowing Gallery

In addition to seeing beautiful hand blown glass floats, ornaments, lamp shades, artwork and more, visitors to the Ocean Beaches Glassblowing Gallery can make their way towards the back where they can watch the glass blowing process almost every *afternoon* and ask questions.

Ocean Beaches Glassblowing Gallery
11175 US-101
Seal Rock, OR 97376
541-563-8632

- Summer: Mon. through Sun. - 9:00 a.m. to 6:00 p.m.
- Winter: Mon. through Thurs. - 10:00 a.m. to 6:00 p.m., Friday through Sunday - 9:00 a.m. to 6:00 p.m.

☐ Seal Rock State Recreation Site

Seal Rock offers a beautiful view of the ocean, as well as seals, sea lions, birds and other marine life. You'll find beach access with tidepools to the south of the parking lot.

Seal Rock State Recreation Site
10032 NW Hwy 101
Seal Rock, OR 97376

Located approximately 10 miles south of Newport on Hwy 101.

WALDPORT, OR

☐ **Waldport Heritage Museum**

Located in a former camp barracks built by the Civilian Conservation Corp in 1941, the Waltport Heritage Museum today offers an interesting collection of items reflecting the history of Waltport, OR and the surrounding area.

Admission is free, but donations are gladly accepted.

> Waltport Heritage Museum
> 320 Northeast Grant Street
> Waltport, OR 97394
> 541-563-7092

* Open: Thursday through Sunday – 12:00 p.m. to 4:00 p.m. (10:00 a.m. to 4:00 p.m. on Saturdays)

☐ **Crabbing in Waldport/The Dock of the Bay Marina**

One of the better places to crab on the Oregon coast, Waldport offers up only tasty Dungeness crab. No "lowly" rock crabs can be found here.

Stop in at the Dock of the Bay Marina and talk to the nice folks there, and they'll get you all set up to go crabbing. You can rent a crab ring for $10 for a 24 hour rental if you'd like to crab off the nearby docks, or go with their "Special" and rent a boat. With this, you'll get a 15' easy-to-start motor boat plus 3 rings with 3 baits for 3 hours, $90. Cooking and cleaning of crabs is also available.

Dock of the Bay Marina
145 NE Mill Street
Waldport, OR 97394
541-563-2003

- Open: Hours can vary with the tides and weather, but The Dock of the Bay Marina is typically open 8:00 a.m. to 4:00 p.m.

YACHATS, OR

☐ The Drift Inn & Cafe

Stop at the historic and award-winning Drift Inn & Cafe, right on the edge of Hwy 101, and step inside for a tasty meal served by nice folks. While enjoying your breakfast cinnamon roll, lunchtime burger, or dinner entrée, be sure to read all about the inn's  colorful and rowdy history on the back of the menu. Afterwards, take the time to walk out the end of the entrance hallway and explore a bit around the "campus" of buildings that make up the inn.

The Drift Inn & Cafe
124 US-101
Yachats, OR 97498
541-547-4477

- Open for breakfast, lunch and dinner

- Open Monday through Sunday – Summer: 8:00 a.m. to 10:00 p.m. – Winter: 8:00 a.m. to 9:00 p.m.

☐ Little Log Church and Museum

It's not often you'll find a museum within a church, but you'll find one in Yachats at the Little Log Church by the Sea. Built in the shape of a cross, this small church was dedicated in 1930, but with its congregation moving to a larger church in 1969, it is today operated as a museum by the Oregon Historical Society. Inside, you'll find the church lovingly preserved along with an interesting collection of items from Yachats' history. The museum is free, but donations are gladly accepted.

Little Log Church Museum
328 W 3rd Street
Yachats, OR 97498
541-547-4547

☐ Yachats Farmers Market

Located one block north of the Little Log Church Museum, the Yachats Farmers Market is a friendly small town market offering an abundance of locally grown and crafted goods.

Yachats Farmers Market
237 4th Street
Yachats, OR 97498

- Open: Sundays – 9:00 a.m. to 2:00 p.m. – Runs from May until the Mushroom Festival in late-October.

CAPE PERPETUA SCENIC AREA

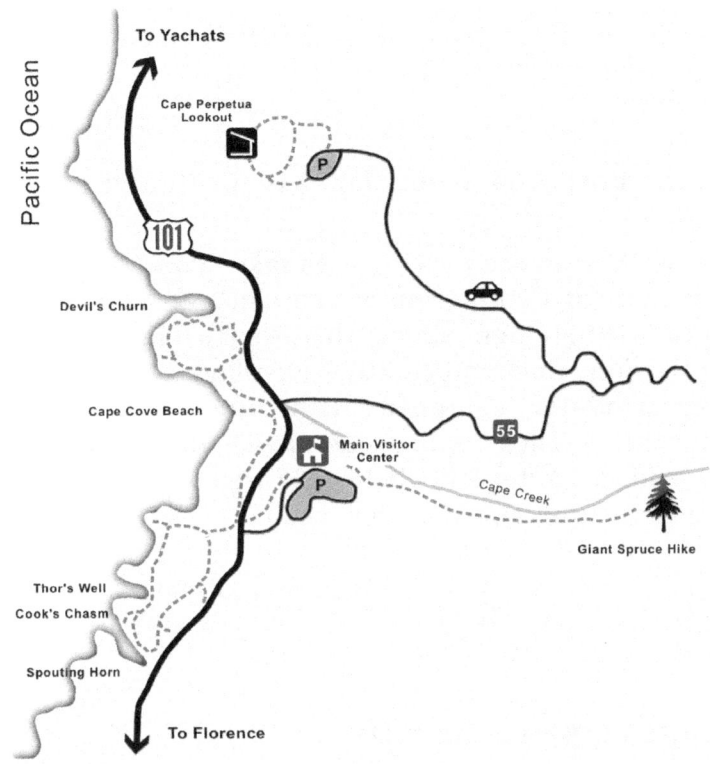

Cape Perpetua is a must-see destination. Geologic wonders, stunning ocean views, an enclosed whale watching facility, a bit of history, and just a touch of danger await at this highlight of the Oregon coast.

Note: Much of Cape Perpetua can be seen with a short stroll, but to see Devil's Churn, Cook's Chasm, Thor's Well, Spouting Horn, the historic CCC structure, and more up close, you'll need to hike a bit.

Driving Directions: The Cape Perpetua Scenic Area includes a couple of stops along Hwy 101, with the largest being at the main visitor center. If you plan on hiking, we recommend that you do not stop at the Devil's Churn Scenic Overlook, (2.6

Miles south of Yachats, OR) as parking is somewhat limited. Instead, park at the main Cape Perpetua Visitor Center (a short distance south of the Devil's Churn Scenic Overlook) and walk north to see Devil's Churn up close. If you do not plan on hiking, then by all means stop at the Devil's Churn overlook and see this interesting Oregon feature.

☐ Cape Perpetua Stop: Main Visitor Center

A short walk from the parking area takes you to the main Cape Perpetua Visitor Center, where you can watch for whales in a park-like setting high above the ocean. Inside the Visitor Center, you'll find interpretive displays, as well as large viewing windows equipped with binoculars for spotting passing Gray Whales. Numerous paved trails from the Visitor Center lead to the features below, as well as viewing platforms and viewpoints overlooking the ocean.

Directions: The turnoff for the Cape Perpetua Main Visitor Center is 3 miles south of Yachats, on Highway 101.

☐ Cape Perpetua Stop: Devil's Churn

 You'll find hiking maps for your next few stops at the Main Visitor Center. From here, follow a trail north to the overlook above Devil's Churn and see how this feature got its name. Afterwards, either make your way back to the Main Visitor Center and then follow the trail towards the tidepools, Thor's Well, the Spouting Horn, and Cook's Chasm, or, *provided ocean conditions allow*, descend the trail at Devil's Churn towards the beach and then make your way south to these attractions on the sand and rock.

Note: Ask at the Visitor Center today when high tide will be and make a note of this, since you'll have the opportunity to walk on the beach and stand near Thor's Well and Cook's Chasm, which are very close to the ocean waves.

☐ Cape Perpetua Stop: Thor's Well

Located at the water's edge is a large gaping barnacle and mussel encrusted hole perhaps 20' across that violently fills with water with each crashing wave from the ocean. Shooting through an opening at its base, the water instantly fills the well and often splashes over the top in dramatic fashion, only to quickly flush back out. It's a truly unique feature of the Oregon Coast.

Note: There is no railing or viewing platform here, and Thor's Well begs you to come closer to get that great photo, but one could easily be swept into the well with no warning, so be mindful of the distance you and little ones keep from the well.

☐ Cape Perpetua Stop: Cook's Chasm

As with Devil's Churn, though on a smaller scale, waves roll into Cook's Chasm from the sea, creating an ever-roiling display of churning and splashing water.

www.Discover-Oregon.com

☐ Cape Perpetua Stop: Spouting Horn

Like Thor's Well, the Spouting Horn is located within the rock right at the water's edge, and with just the right wave action, water rushes into the "horn" and sprays high into the air.

☐ Cape Perpetua Stop: 1933 CCC Lookout Shelter Atop Cape Perpetua

High above the Visitor Center, atop Cape Perpetua, is the West Shelter, a small stone structure built by the Civilian Conservation Corps. Standing 800' above the ocean, it holds a

commanding view of over 100 miles of coastline, as well as looks out over 37 miles to the horizon. Built in the summer of 1933, today it is a popular location for picnicking, whale watching, and getting married.

Note: If the weather is agreeable, the south facing slope atop Cape Perpetua is *the* perfect spot to sit down and enjoy lunch with a commanding view.

Driving Directions: From the Cape Perpetua Visitor Center, return to Hwy 101 and drive *north* for 0.3 mile to road NFD-55, which leads to the Cape Perpetua Day Use Campground. Turn right / east here and proceed 0.8 mile to Cape Perpetua Lookout Road. Turn left here and follow this 0.9 mile to the Cape Perpetua Lookout parking area. Be sure to take the pathway to the south to see the amazing view and then wind your way north to find the historic CCC shelter.

HECETA HEAD LIGHTHOUSE

☐ **Heceta Head Lighthouse & Viewpoint**

The Oregon Coast offers an opportunity to visit one of the most beautiful and most photographed lighthouses in the world. Perched out on Heceta Head is the majestic Heceta Head Lighthouse. With a history reaching back to 1894, it still dutifully performs its task today, guiding ships to safety along the Oregon Coast.

Make your way along a trail from the parking area out to the lighthouse and its scenic viewpoint, where you may take a tour to learn about the history of the lighthouse, its construction, and its role today on the Oregon Coast. In addition, be sure to take the trail that leads near the Heceta Head Lighthouse Keeper's House, a restored 1893 home, which today serves as a bed and breakfast. As a bed and breakfast, it is open only to those who are staying there. See page 97 for additional information.

- Lighthouse tours are given seven days a week, from 11:00 a.m. to 3:00 p.m. Tours are given until only 2:00 p.m. during the winter, weather and staff permitting.

- To capture a photo of the lighthouse from above, take the short trail which leads up the hill behind the lighthouse to a small viewpoint.

- Day-use parking permits ($5) are required at Heceta Head Lighthouse State Scenic Viewpoint and may be purchased from a machine at the park. Note that parking is located south of the lighthouse, off a road leading from Highway 101. See the map below.

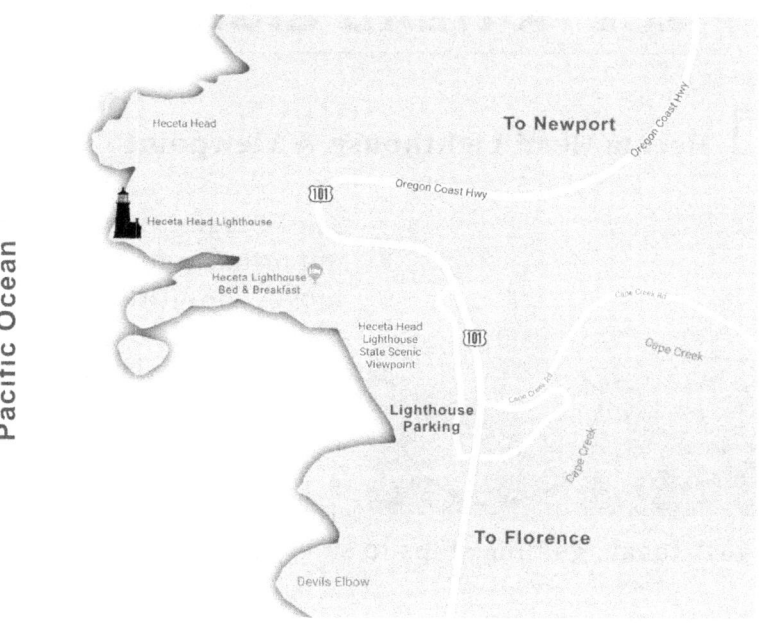

www.Discover-Oregon.com

Heceta Head Lighthouse Bed & Breakfast

Standing majestically upon Heceta Head is the Heceta Head Lighthouse, recognized as one of the most beautiful lighthouses in the world. Built in 1894, its powerful beacon still shines today, casting its beam 21 miles out to sea, thus making it the brightest light on the Oregon Coast.

Perched high on a cliff only a short stroll inland is the historic Heceta Head Lighthouse Keeper's House. Owned by the Oregon State Parks division, this stately home is managed as a fine bed and breakfast, offering seven rooms, private baths, spacious grounds, and a casual yet formal 7-course breakfast.

Each room offers a victorian theme, with the Queen Anne Room offering romantic accomodations, the highly sought

Lightkeeper's room offering a view of the lighthouse from the bed, and the Mariners Room I offering accomodations said to be haunted. (Though we didn't find that to be the case when we stayed there!)

Enjoy a good night's sleep, wake up and enjoy your breakfast, learn all about the history of the home with a quick tour, and then stroll out to the lighthouse for a panoramic ocean view.

Heceta Head Lighthouse Bed & Breakfast
92072 US-101
Yachats, OR 97498
541-547-3696
1-866-547-3696
www.HecetaLighthouse.com

☐ An Iconic View of Heceta Head

At 0.8 mile south of the Heceta Head Lighthouse is a paved parking area just off of Highway 101. Pull in here and look back north to enjoy a beautiful view of the Heceta Head Lighthouse. It is because of this view that the Heceta Head Lighthouse is the most photographed lighthouse on the Oregon Coast.

SEA LION CAVES, FLORENCE, OREGON DUNES, REEDSPORT, WINCHESTER BAY & COOS BAY

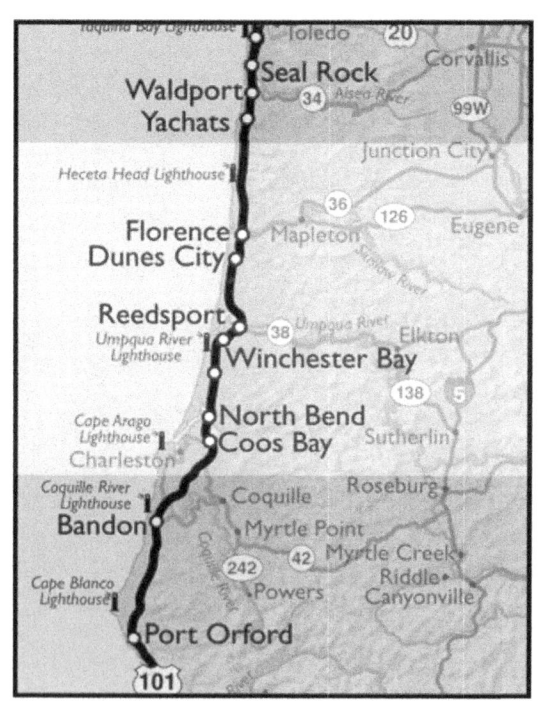

☐ Sea Lion Caves

In 1880, Captain William Cox was exploring the calm seas of the Pacific Ocean aboard a small craft 11 miles north of Florence, Oregon when he came upon the opening to an immense cave. Taking advantage of the rare ocean conditions, he entered the cave and found it to be approximately 100 yards deep and over 125 feet high. What he had discovered was the largest sea cave in America, and one that was home to hundreds of sea lions.

Today, Sea Lion Caves is a privately owned wildlife preserve and bird sanctuary, which is part of the Cape Perpetua Marine Reserve. Here, Stellar Sea Lions by the hundreds rest deep in the caves during the stormy winter months and then move out to the rock ledges near the entrance of the cave during the warmer and calmer spring and summer months.

Visitors can conveniently descend 208 feet to the cave below via an elevator, though you will need to descend 37 stair steps and walk 400 yards down a steep grade to reach the elevator. Once in the cave, you'll need to navigate 63 additional stair steps to reach the lighthouse viewpoint. Note that you'll need to retrace your steps to return to the parking area.

Admission:

Adults:	$14.00
Seniors:	$13.00
Ages 5 to 12:	$8.00
Ages 4 and Under:	Free

Sea Lion Caves
91560 US Hwy 101
Florence, OR 97439
541-547-3111

- Open: Monday through Sunday – 9:00 a.m. to 5:00 p.m. Open every day of the year, except for Thanksgiving and Christmas Day, weather permitting.

FLORENCE, OR

 ☐ **Florence, Oregon – Old Town District**

Located just north of the 1936 Siuslaw River Bridge with art deco styling is the quaint beach town of Florence, Oregon. Be sure to visit the "Old Town" district, with its many different shops catering to tourists, including coffee shops, gift shops, bookstores, a bakery, an art gallery, a Mo's Seafood & Chowder house, various restaurants and more.

☐ Edwin K Bed & Breakfast

Just a few blocks west of the old town area is the Edwin K Bed & Breakfast. Walk on over to take a look at this restored 1914 Sears Craftsman home and stop in to get a sense of its charms so you'll know of another great place to stay for a future road trip or weekend  visit to Florence and the Oregon Coast.

Edwin K Bed & Breakfast
1155 Bay Street
Florence, OR 97439
541-997-8360

☐ Siuslaw Pioneer Museum

Visit the Siuslaw Pioneer Museum to discover the natural and cultural history of the area, as well as learn about the lives of those who "lived, died, worked and played in the greater Siuslaw River Basin."

For those who would like a bit more immersive history, take the self-guided Historic Walking Tour, which leaves from the museum and visits 21 different buildings and locations in the Old Town Florence area.

Siuslaw Pioneer Museum
278 Maple Street
Florence, OR 97439
541-997-7884

- Open: Monday through Sunday – 12:00 p.m. to 4:00 p.m.

☐ Oregon Coast Military Museum

Dedicated to honoring those citizens, past and present, who have bravely served our country, this impressively curated museum displays a collection of life-sized dioramas and exhibits that depict scenes from military service since World War I, as well as artifacts, memorabilia, equipment, photos and more.

Oregon Coast Military Museum
2145 Kingwood Street
Florence, OR 97439
541-902-5160

- Open: Wednesday through Sunday – 12:00 p.m. to 4:00 p.m. – General Admission: $5.00 – Kids 12 and under: Free

☐ Apex Helicopters – See the Oregon Coast by Air!

You've seen the Oregon Coast by car, now see its spectacular beauty by air! Take to the skies aboard an Apex Helicopter to spot Gray Whales, see the Sea Lion Caves, experience a unique view of Heceta Head Lighthouse, soar over the rugged Oregon coast line and capes, and so much more. Tours aboard a climate controlled helicopter are offered 7 days a week, year-round. Nine different tours are available, beginning at $125 per person, for 2 to 4 people. Custom tours are also available.

Apex Helicopters
2001 Airport Way
Florence, OR 97439
541-997-3270

☐ Oregon Dunes National Recreation Area

While you'll find stretches of sandy beaches all along the Oregon Coast, you won't find anything like the Oregon Dunes National Recreation Area. Here, great expanses of sand are sculpted by the wind into hills, bowls and steep slopes for 40 miles along the coastline, stretching from the Siuslaw River in

Florence down to the Coos River in North Bend. This unique coastal landscape appeals to hikers, photographers, birders, and others, but the real action happens with the dune buggies and sand rails that race over the dunes with amazing speed, offering riders a unique Oregon experience filled with thrills and excitement.

Spanning 40 miles, you'll find numerous observation areas and trailheads along the Oregon Dunes National Recreation Area, such as at the Jessie M. Honeyman Memorial State Park, (4 miles south of Florence) the Oregon Dunes Overlook, (11 miles south of Florence) and the John Dellenback Dunes Trail, (10.5 miles south of Reedsport). Dune buggy and sand rail tours are available through a number of companies, including those listed on the following pages.

☐ Sand Dunes Road

For an interesting, albeit short, Oregon Coast excursion, take a drive on Sand Dunes Road as it makes its way north through 6 miles of sand dunes to the mouth of the Siuslaw River.

Driving Directions: You'll find South Jetty Rd. / Sand Dunes Rd. south of Florence and 0.6 miles south of the Siuslaw River. Turn west here and follow the road west and then north to the *South Jetty Dunes and Beach.*

☐ Guided Sand Rail Tours

It's time to put on your goggles, feel the breeze in your hair, and fill your shoes with sand!

Stretching 40 miles from Florence, OR down to Coos Bay, OR is the Oregon Dunes National Recreation Area, where the wind sculpts the ever-changing sand dunes into hills, bowls, plateaus, and ridges, sometimes reaching up to 500'

high! And what better way to experience them than aboard a sand rail, a lightweight off-road and on-sand vehicle designed for high-speed thrills on the Oregon dunes.

We loved roaring across the sand, dropping over high lips, racing down steep faces, hitting exhilarating (though minor) jumps, and throwing rooster tails of sand the entire way. No doubt you will, too.

There are a few different tour providers on the coast, and here are two we'd recommend:

Sandland Adventures

Tours: ½ Hour Tour: $35 per person – 1 Hour Tour: $65 per person. Tours run rain or shine, so dress accordingly. Reservations are recommended, but not necessary. No refunds are given on tours within 72 hours of departure.

> Sandland Adventures
> 85366 Highway 101
> Florence, OR 97439
> 541-997-8087
> www.SandLand.com

Summer Hours:

> Monday through Friday – 9:00 a.m. to 5:00 p.m. with extended summer hours – Memorial Day weekend through September – Closed the first 4 days after Labor Day Monday.

Winter Hours:

> Tuesday through Saturday – 9:00 a.m. to 5:00 p.m. – October through December and March to Memorial Day Weekend.

Sand Dunes Frontier

Tours: ½ Hour Tour: $35 per person – 1 Hour tours during the off season: $65 per person. The last trip in the summer typically leaves sometime between 6:30 p.m. and 7:00 p.m. Trips go out rain or shine, and are first come, first served.

> Sand Dunes Frontier
> 83960 Hwy 101
> Florence, OR 97439
> 541-997-3544
> www.SandDunesFrontier.com

Summer Hours:

> Monday through Friday – 9:00 a.m. to 6:00 p.m.

Winter Hours:
> Tuesday through Saturday - December 15 to March 15 - 10:00 a.m. to 4:00 p.m.

REEDSPORT, OR

☐ **Umpqua Discovery Center**

Experience the natural and cultural history of the Lower Umpqua Area through hands-on interpretive displays at the Umpqua Discovery Center. Here, you'll learn about the Kuuich Indians, the early pioneers, the important role logging played in this area, the natural history of the tidewater country, and much more.

Admission: Adults: $8.00 – Children (5-16): $4.00

> Umpqua Discovery Center
> 409 Riverfront Way
> Reedsport, OR 97467
> 541-271-4816

Summer Hours:

Monday through Saturday – 10:00 a.m. to 5:00 p.m. – Sunday 12:00 p.m. to 4:00 p.m.

Winter Hours:

Monday through Saturday – 10:00 a.m. to 4:00 p.m. – Sunday 12:00 p.m. to 4:00 p.m.

☐ Dean Creek Elk Viewing Area

 Make a short 3.7 mile drive east of Reedsport, OR on Hwy 38 / the Umpqua River Scenic Byway to the Dean Creek Elk Viewing Area to see views of majestic Roosevelt Elk. While there is no guarantee the elk will be there at the time of your visit, the herd here can reach as many as 120 animals in size, and they are often seen early in the morning and at dusk.

Dean Creek Elk Viewing Area
48819 OR-38
Reedsport, OR 97467
541-756-0100

Winchester Bay, OR – Umpqua River Lighthouse

☐ Umpqua River Light House & Museum

Initially built in 1857 near the mouth of the Umpqua River, and then rebuilt in 1894, the Umpqua River Lighthouse is a majestic though somewhat elusive piece of the Oregon Coast's history. Off limits behind a chain link fence, the 65' tall lighthouse with its distinctive red lens may only be accessed as part of a tour.

To arrange a tour of the lighthouse, visit the Douglas County Museum located one block to the north. Note that no tours are available after 4:00 p.m.

> Umpqua River Lighthouse & Museum
> 1020 Lighthouse Road
> Winchester Bay, OR 97467
> 541-271-4631

- Open: Monday through Sunday – 10:00 a.m. to 4:00 p.m.

Coos Bay, OR

☐ Coos History Museum & Maritime Collection

The "anchor" of your visits while in Coos Bay is the impressive Coos History Museum & Maritime Collection. Showcasing the maritime, agricultural, and cultural history of the Coos Bay area and south Oregon coast, the museum's displays explore the lives of the area's first inhabitants, as well as those of the early pioneers, and take a look at the logging, fishing and seafaring industries which helped to shape the region. In addition, visitors will find in the foyer an interesting display dedicated to noted  Oregon middle and long-distance runner Steve Prefontaine, who lived in Coos Bay.

Coos History Museum
1210 North Front Street
Coos Bay, OR 97420
541-756-6320

• Open: Tuesday through Sunday – 10:00 a.m. to 5:00 p.m.

☐ Marshfield Sun Printing Museum

 After visiting the Coos History Museum, walk over to the small Marshfield Sun Printing Museum building. Inside, you'll find the original antique printing presses, type cases, imposing tables, and other equipment, all arranged in its original layout, which was used in the printing of The Sun newspaper from 1891 to 1944. Admission is free, but donations are accepted.

Marshfield Sun Printing Museum
1049 North Front Street
Coos Bay, OR 97420
541-266-0901

- Open: Tuesday through Saturday – 1:00 p.m. to 4:00 p.m. – Memorial Day to Labor Day – Personal tours are available by appointment all year.

Walking Directions: If you're visiting the Coos History Museum, then it's just a short walk southeast over to the Marshfield Sun Printing Museum.

☐ Oregon Coast Historical Railway

Situated behind a black iron fence next to Hwy 101 in Coos Bay is the growing collection of the Oregon Coast Historical Railway. A smartly painted 1922 Baldwin steam locomotive dominates the yard, and it's joined by a 1949 Alco S-2 diesel switcher engine, a 1942 steel caboose, a 1946-era wooden caboose, and an abundance of historical railroading and logging equipment.

Oregon Coast Historical Railway
800 South 1st Street
Coos Bay, OR 97420
541-267-6900

- Open: Wednesday *and* Saturday – 9:00 a.m. to 3:00 p.m.

☐ Coos Bay Farmers Market

Browse over 60 vendors to find the best of the south Oregon Coast. Fresh produce and vegetables, eggs, honey, baked goods, coffee, jams and jellies, fresh meats, handmade crafts, baked goods and more await shoppers every Wednesday all summer long.

Coos Bay Farmers Market
Heart of the Marshfield District
Central Avenue – Between Hwy 101 and 4th Ave.
541-266-9711

- Open: Every Wednesday – 9:00 a.m. to 2:00 p.m. – May through October

Charleston to Bandon Scenic Tour Route, Cape Arago Beach Loop, Shore Acres State Park & Bandon

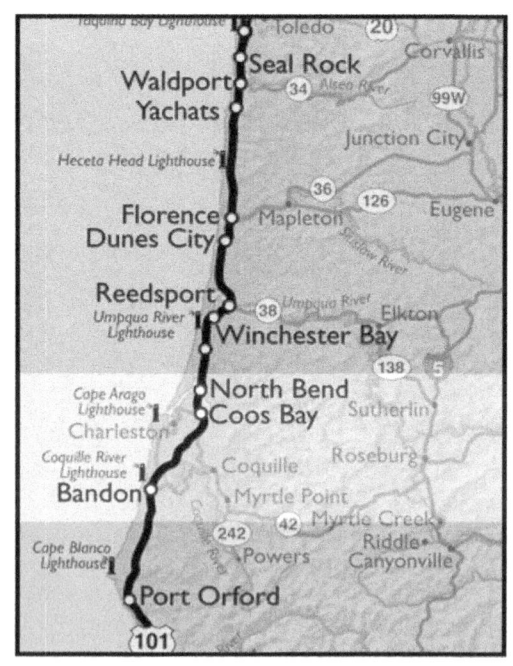

CHARLESTON TO BANDON
SCENIC TOUR ROUTE

Pacific Ocean

North Bend

Cooston

Newmark Ave

Coos Bay

Barview

Bunker Hill

Sunset Bay
State Park

Charleston

Shore Acres
State Park

Millington

Cape Arago
State Park

Seven Devils Rd.

South Slough
National
Estuarine
Research...

W. Beaver Hill Rd.

Seven Devils
State Rec. Park

Whiskey Run Rd.

Leneve

Bandon Dunes
Golf Resort

Cedar Point   Coquille

Bullards Beach
State Park

Randolph

Riverton

Bullards

Parkersburg

Charleston to Bandon

Scenic Tour Route

Coquille River
Lighthouse

Bandon

Like the Three Capes Scenic Drive south of Tillamook, the Charleston to Bandon Scenic Tour Route is a meandering 41 mile byway along the scenic cliffs and beaches of the Oregon coastline, west of Hwy 101. Beginning with the Cape Arago Beach Loop, which leads travelers to a string of state parks, the scenic tour route then proceeds south along Seven Devils Road to Bandon, OR, where it then rejoins Highway 101. Along the way it rewards travelers with panoramic ocean vistas, the beautiful landscaped gardens of Shore Acres State Park, a view of the Cape Arago Lighthouse, and the busy activities of over 1,000 seals and sea lions at Simpson Reef Overlook.

Note: The following attractions and driving directions are listed from north to south.

 **First Stop:** Cranberry Sweets & More

Located in both Coos Bay and old town Bandon, Cranberry Sweets & More showcases a bounty of cranberry products made from cranberries grown in the Bandon area, the *Cranberry Capital of Oregon*. Stop in at their Coos Bay factory store where you can watch candy being made during most weekdays, as well as "sample your heart out." Inside, you'll find jelly candies, toffees, brittles, fudge, cookies, caramels, assorted chocolates, salt water taffy, popcorn "& More".

Cranberry Sweets & More
1005 Newmark Ave.
Coos Bay, OR 97420
541-888-9824

- Open: Monday through Saturday – 9:30 a.m. to 5:30 p.m. – Sunday: 11:00 a.m. to 4:00 p.m.

 ☐ **Next Stop:** University of Oregon Charleston Marine Life Center

 Oregon State University has a number of satellite campuses across the state engaged in research, one of which is located right on the harbor in Charleston, OR. Open to the public, the Charleston Marine Life Center welcomes future marine biologists with a touch tank, salt water aquariums holding animals collected from the Oregon coast, (including Octopi) and five exhibit galleries focused on the animals, habitats and ecosystems of the coast.

Admission is $5, and children and students are free.

Charleston Marine Life Center
63466 Boat Basin Road
Charleston, OR 97420
541-888-2581

- Open: Wednesday through Saturday – 11:00 a.m. to 5:00 p.m.

Driving Directions: From Cranberry Sweets & More, drive west on Newmark Ave. for 0.4 mile to where it curves south and becomes the Cape Arago Highway. Continue south from this point for another 4.8 miles into Charleston, and then turn right onto Boat Basin Road, shortly after crossing the bridge. You'll see the U of O Charleston Marine Life Center on your right in 1/2 mile.

 **Next Stop:** Cape Arago Beach Loop

The Charleston to Bandon Scenic Tour Loop begins with a drive on the Cape Arago Beach Loop, which runs north to south as it passes a collection of beautiful state parks above the ocean waters. Along the way, you'll visit:

- Sunset Beach State Park
- Shore Acres State Park
- Simpson Reef Overlook
- Cape Arago Lookout

Upon reaching Cape Arago Lookout, you'll then retrace your route back to the Charleston to Bandon Scenic Tour Route.

 **Next Stop:** Sunset Bay State Park

Visit a scenic sandy beach tucked into a cove protected by rocky sea cliffs. The interpretive center here offers a number of services, including guided tidepool walks, nature walks, living history walks and Junior Ranger programs. Contact the Interpretive Center at 541-888-0982 for times and dates.

Open:

- May through June 15 – Friday through Sunday: 9:15 a.m. to 5:00 p.m.

- June 16 through September 15 – Open daily: 9:15 a.m. to 5:00 p.m.

Driving Directions: From the Charleston Marine Life Center, return to the Cape Arago Hwy and turn right / west. Follow this for 0.3 mile to where it turns into the Cape Arago Beach Loop. Continue to the 2.9 mile mark, where you'll find parking for Sunset Beach State Park.

 **Next Stop:** Shore Acres State Park

 The weather and temperature on the Oregon Coast is perfect for growing plants during much of the year, so it's a bit of a wonder as to why there aren't more formal gardens dotting the coast. Shore Acres State Park  certainly answers the call, as here travelers will find the beautifully landscaped grounds of a former lumber baron's estate. Walk the pathways, make your way through the boxwood lined flower gardens, wander to the quiet pond, visit the rose garden, and discover an abundance of plants blooming in a myriad colors, a few of which you may have never seen before in your life.

 Afterwards, make your way to the large observation building or walk the path along the cliff top to see the rugged shoreline below, one of the most dramatic on the Oregon Coast, especially in rough weather. Don't forget to keep an eye out for whales.

Note: An Oregon State Parks Pass or fee is required here.

Driving Directions: From Sunset Beach State Park, proceed along the Cape Arago Beach Loop for 1.1 miles to the entrance for Shore Acres State Park.

 ☐ **Next Stop:** Simpson Reef Overlook

 Simpson Reef Overlook is a fascinating and scenic "must stop". Here, the gradual slope of the offshore rocks and sandy beaches make this area the best location on the Oregon Coast for Stellar Sea Lions, California Sea Lions, Harbor Seals, and Northern Elephant Seals to "haul out", lay in the sun, and bark at each other. You'll likely hear over 1,000 of them out on the reef as soon as you get out of your car. Don't forget your binoculars.

Driving Directions: Continue on the Cape Arago Beach Loop for 1.0 mile to the Simpson Reef Overlook.

 ☐ **Next Stop:** Cape Arago State Park

 Continue 0.8 mile south to Cape Arago State Park to enjoy a stunning panoramic ocean view from a stone wall overlook on a bluff high above the ocean waves.

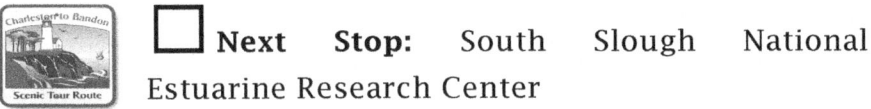

☐ Next Stop: South Slough National Estuarine Research Center

An important part of Oregon's marine ecosystem, the salt flats, mud flats and channels of the South Slough provide a home for young Dungeness crab, oysters, shellfish, salmon and herring, as well as a varied collection of sea birds. Stop in at the South Slough National Estuarine Research Center to learn all about the South Slough through its impressive interpretive displays, as well as its collection of 10 short hikes ranging from .17 to .75 miles in length. In addition, be sure to say "Hello" to Ophelia, the Dungeness crab in the large saltwater tank in the entrance. A bit gregarious for a crab, don't be surprised if she comes to the front glass to greet you, which is nice, because we usually find Dungeness crabs to be a bit standoffish.

South Slough National Estuarine Research Center
61907 Seven Devils Road
Charleston, OR 97420
541-888-5558

• Open: Tuesday through Saturday – 10:00 a.m. to 4:30 p.m.

Driving Directions: From the Cape Arago Lookout, retrace your drive back north on the Cape Arago Beach Loop for 5.5 miles to Seven Devils Road. Turn right here and proceed south for another 4.2 miles to the entrance for the South Slough National Estuarine Research Center, on your left.

 ☐ **Next Stop:** Seven Devils Beach

If you're looking for a walk on a nice beach, then Seven Devils Beach is just the ticket. At 5.5 miles in length, it's a wide open expanse of shoreline just waiting to be explored. Note that the beach running north from the Coquille Lighthouse (your next stop) is a nice long beach, as well.

Driving Directions: From the South Slough National Estuarine Research Center, return to Seven Devils Road and turn left / south. Continue on Seven Devils Road for 6.5 miles (which becomes W Beaver Hill Road) to Whiskey Run Road / E Humphreys Road. Turn right / west here and continue on this for 2.5 miles as it connects again with Seven Devils Road. Turn right / north here and follow this for 1.6 miles to the left turn for Seven Devils Beach.

 ☐ **Next Stop:** Bullards Beach State Park & Coquille River Lighthouse

The drive from Hwy 101 through Bullards Beach State Park out to the Coquille River Lighthouse is a beautiful drive, which reminds us a little bit of portions of 17-Mile Drive along the Monterey Peninsula in California. Passing through the very nice and aptly awarded "All Star" Bullards Beach State Park, the drive continues into the open along a spit of sand with the ocean just beyond the passenger side window. Soon, it finishes in a turnaround at the historic and picturesque 1896 Coquille Lighthouse, next to the Coquille River jetty.

Visitors are welcome to tour the lighthouse from 11:00 a.m. to 5:00 p.m., mid-May through September, when it is staffed with volunteers. The tower, however, is off limits due to safety concerns. For additional information, you may call the park office at 541-347-2209.

The 4.5 mile long beach stretching north from here is very nice for walking, and the jetty itself is also an interesting stroll, though it can be dangerous. Do not walk out on it if the seas are rough or the surface is wet! Also, do not

turn your back on the ocean. Note that there are a few picnic tables by the lighthouse, and this is a nice spot to enjoy a bite while watching fishing trawlers making their way out to sea and back.

For you photographers, you may find it handy to take photos of the lighthouse from the west. Position the small structure to the west of the base of the lighthouse within your frame such that it appears to be the base of the lighthouse tower.

Driving Directions: From Seven Devils Beach, return south on Seven Devils Road for 3.5 miles to Randolph Road. Turn left / east here and follow Randolph Road for 1.7 miles as it makes its way straight across Hwy 101 and meets up with N Bank Ln. Turn right here and follow this for 2.5 miles to Hwy 101. Turn right / *north* onto Hwy 101 and follow this for 0.1 mile before turning left / west onto Bullards Beach Road. Continue on this road for 3 miles as it makes its way through the State Park to the Coquille River Lighthouse. (We took you the scenic way!)

BANDON, OR

Home of the Bandon Cranberry Festival, this jewel of a small coastal town offers visitors a lively historic district, a collection of interesting shops and galleries, a truly unique museum, world-class chocolates, and the perfect place to catch and savor your own Dungeness crab.

 **Tony's Crab Shack**

If it's time to eat, then Tony's Crab Shack is the place. Though its menu offers a wide selection of fresh seafood items, including ocean shrimp, wild prawns, local oysters, salmon, halibut, clams and much more, which are *"Always fresh - never fried."*, Tony's is known for its fresh Dungeness crab. Grab a table inside or out (you may have to wait a bit) and enjoy some fresh Oregon seafood while watching all the busy activity right on the water's edge.

Tony's Crab Shack
155 1st Street SE
Bandon, OR 97411
541-347-2875

- Open Monday through Sunday – 10:30 a.m. to 7:00 p.m. during the summer. Until 6:00 p.m. in winter.

 If you've never gone crabbing on the Oregon Coast, then now is the perfect time...and place...to give it a try, and whether you're a complete novice or seasoned pro, Tony's is more than happy to help out with all the equipment, advice, and tips you'll need to enjoy this iconic Oregon experience.

Attached to the restaurant is Tony's Port O' Call Tackle and Gifts, a one-stop shop for your  crabbing rentals. Here, you can buy a one-day crabbing license and rent a crab ring or trap, complete with a bucket and bait, for crabbing off the nearby docks, or if you're feeling a bit more adventurous you can also rent a small boat for crabbing in the bay. Once you've hauled in your catch, head the crew back to Tony's and they'll cook each crab for only $0.75 cents each, and for $3.00 each, they'll set you up with a plate, napkin, utensils, and a bit of melted butter to enjoy your meal.

 Before you begin, Tony's will give you plenty of advice, as well as a read on the current crabbing conditions. In a nutshell, crabbing is best one hour before to one hour after high tide, and if it hasn't rained lately, then all the better, as the bay will have less freshwater running through it. Be sure to allot at least two hours of time for your crabbing and ensuing meal.

 **Washed Ashore Gallery**

This is a "must see" attraction when you are in Bandon. Not only is its message important, but the large intricate works of art they create from ocean trash to educate a global audience about the extent of plastic pollution is downright amazing.

Washed Ashore Gallery & Workshop
325 2nd Street SE
Bandon, OR 97411
541-329-0317

Summer Hours:

- Mid-June through mid-September – Tuesday through Saturday 11:00 a.m. to 5:00 p.m.

Winter Hours:

- Mid-September through mid-June – Thursday through Saturday – 12:00 p.m. to 5:00 p.m.

www.Discover-Oregon.com

 ☐ **Coastal Mist Chocolates**

Every trip to the Oregon Coast should involve chocolate, and while in Bandon you'll find it at Coastal Mist Chocolates in the Old Town area. Savor their world-class artisan chocolates, European style desserts and pastries, gourmet sandwiches, decadent truffles and more.

Coastal Mist Chocolates
210 2nd Street SE
Bandon, OR 97411
541-347-3300

- Open: Monday through Thursday – 11:00 a.m. to 5:30 p.m., Friday and Saturday – 10:00 a.m. to 6:00 p.m., and Sunday – 10:00 a.m. to 5:00 p.m.

 ☐ **Bandon Historical Society Museum**

Housed in the former Bandon City Hall, the second building built after the great fire of 1936, the Bandon Historical Society Museum contains a wealth of items which showcase the city's history, tragic shipwrecks, industries that shaped Bandon's past, and the cultural and natural history of the region.

Bandon Historical Society Museum
270 Fillmore Ave. SE
Bandon, OR 97411
541-347-2164

- Open: Monday through Friday – 10:00 a.m. to 4:00 p.m.

 ☐ **Face Rock Creamery**

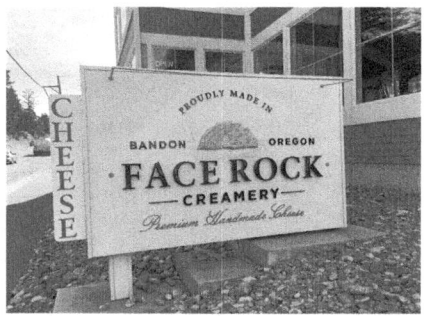

Visit the Face Rock Creamery to see how their award-winning cheeses are made, as well as sample an abundance of different cheeses, some hand-scooped ice cream, tasty chocolates, and more.

Face Rock Creamery
680 2nd Street SE
Bandon, OR 97411
541-347-3223

- Open: Monday through Sunday – 9:00 a.m. to 6:00 p.m.

 ☐ **Coquille Point & The Bandon Sea Stacks**

Stop at Coquille Point and enjoy a beautiful 180 degree view of Bandon's many sea stacks, including Table Rock, Five Foot Rock, Sisters, Wash Rock and Face Rock, which is only ½ mile to the south. In addition, make your way down the long staircase to the beach below during low tide and walk amongst the sea stacks or take a walk on the flat paved interpretive trail found at the top of the stairs.

Driving Directions: From Bandon, drive west on Hwy 101 for approximately 0.5 miles as it curves to the south, and then turn right / west onto 11th Street SW. Follow this west through the City Park for 1 mile to the parking area and viewpoint.

 ☐ **Face Rock Viewpoint**

Like some surreal sculpture, Bandon's Face Rock looks just like a human face forever locked in a skyward gaze. It's uncanny how geologic chance captured this "look", which becomes even more apparent with the shadows of later in the day.

Driving Directions: From Coquille Point, return east 1 block to Beach Loop Road and turn right. Proceed 0.6 mile to Face Rock.

☐ **West Coast Game Park Safari**

 Located just south of Bandon on US-101 is the West Coast Game Park Safari, a walk-through safari park where visitors can view, interact with, and photograph over 450 animals, including African Lions, Bengal Tigers, Snow

Leopards, cougars, bears, zebras, bison, camels, chimpanzees, deer and many others. Springtime is especially fun, as it provides once-in-a-lifetime opportunities to interact with young lions, tigers, leopards and other wild animals. Plan on taking about one hour here.

Rates range from $9.00 to $19.00. Children under 2 are free.

West Coast Game Park Safari
46914 US-101
Bandon, OR 97411
541-347-3106

- Open: Monday through Sunday – 10:00 a.m. to 5:00 p.m. Note: Last entry is at 4:30 p.m.

☐ New River Nature Center

Located up a short road off of Highway 101, this small but impressive nature center explains the habitats and ecosystems of the nearby New River Area of Critical Environmental Concern, an area offering miles of trails, waterways, and beaches for exploring.

New River Nature Center
86434-86442 Croft Lake Road
Bandon, OR 97411

☐ Dragonfly Farm & Nursery

Part of the Wild Rivers Coast Farm Trail, which runs from Bandon, OR to Port Orford, OR and supplies local vendors with local farm produce for visitors to enjoy, Dragonfly Farm offers a large variety of unique and indigenous plants, all in a setting surrounded by  tall coastal firs. Stop in to see what's growing on the Oregon Coast, and keep an eye out for the free-roaming chickens!

Dragonfly Farms & Nursery
49295 Highway 101
Langlois, OR 97450
541-844-5559

* Open: Wednesday through Saturday – 10:00 a.m. to 4:00 p.m., Sunday – 11:00 a.m. to 4:00 p.m.

Cape Blanco, Port Orford, Gold Beach, Samuel H. Boardman Scenic Corridor & Brookings

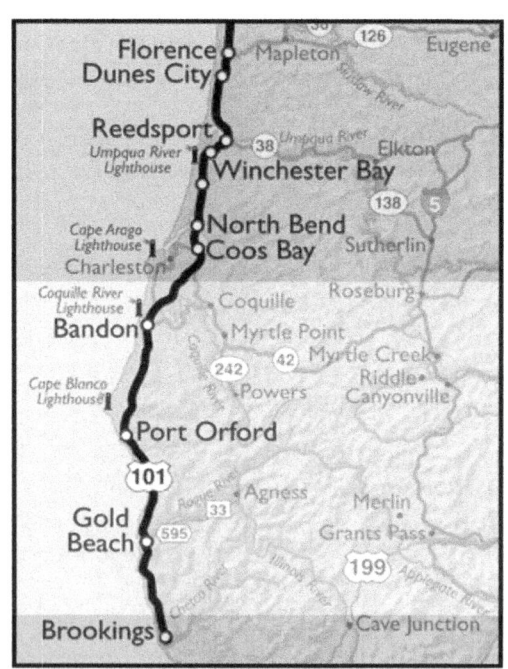

CAPE BLANCO & PORT ORFORD, OR

☐ **Cape Blanco State Park and Cape Blanco Lighthouse**

First lit in December of 1870, the historic Cape Blanco Lighthouse is not only Oregon's southernmost lighthouse, but it also occupies the farthest point west in the state. Visit the nearby gift shop to purchase a ticket for the tour, and learn all about  the lighthouse and the keepers who lived on the cape.

Tickets for lighthouse tours are $2 for adults 16 and older. 15 and under are free of charge.

Cape Blanco Lighthouse
91100 Cape Blanco Road
Port Orford, OR 97465
541-332-2207

- Open: Wednesday through Monday (Closed Tuesdays) – April through October 31st - 10:00 a.m. to 3:15 p.m. The last tour ticket is sold at 3:15, but this doesn't give you enough time to tour the lighthouse and hear about its history. Gates close at 3:30 p.m.

☐ **Patrick Hughes House**

Located within Cape Blanco State Park and just off the drive to the Cape Blanco Lighthouse, is the beautiful 1898 Queen Anne style home of Patrick and Jane Hughes. Restored and well

curated with impressive period-specific furnishings, the home and its volunteers welcome visitors to learn about the Hughes, their lives in the area, and their seven children, one of which was a keeper at the nearby Cape Blanco Lighthouse. Tours are free, but donations are gladly accepted to help fund the continued restoration and maintenance of the home.

Patrick Hughes House
91816 Cape Blanco Road
Port Orford, OR 97465
541-332-0248

- Open: Wednesday through Monday (Closed Tuesdays) – April through October 31st - 10:00 a.m. to 3:30 p.m.

☐ Port Orford Lifeboat Station Museum

Beginning in 1934 and continuing into the 1960s, the Port Orford Lifeboat Station housed Surfmen, who would answer the call of ships in distress by racing down 532 steps to Nellie's Cove and courageously row a rescue boat out into rough seas to save the lives of imperiled sailors. Today, you can visit and tour the museum housed in the former barracks to learn about the role of the Lifeboat Station and the men stationed here. In addition, you can walk the grounds, see a restored 36 foot self-righting lifeboat, and take a hike down to Nellie's Cove. Note: If you'd like a fun souvenir, have a custom dog tag made at the museum.

The museum and tour are free, though donations are gladly accepted.

Port Orford Lifeboat Station
92331 Coast Guard Hill Road
Port Orford, OR 97465
541-332-0521

- Open: Wednesday through Monday (Closed Tuesdays) – April through October 31st - 10:00 a.m. to 3:30 p.m.

☐ The Crazy Norwegian's Fish and Chips

A favorite destination for "locals" all up and down the coast, "Crazy's" offers a large selection of fresh seafood, burgers, soups and salads for lunch and dinner. Don't forget to have some freshly made pie before hitting the road!

The Crazy Norwegian's Fish and Chips
259 6th Street
Port Orford, OR 97465
541-332-8601

- Open: Tuesday through Sunday – 11:30 a.m. to 7:30 p.m.

☐ Prehistoric Gardens

 A fun Oregon Coast attraction with a history reaching back over 70 million years! Wander through an ancient Oregon rainforest past 23 life-size dinosaurs and other prehistoric creatures, including a flying Pteranodon, with its impressive 27' wingspan, a towering Brachiosaurus reaching 46' high, and a terrifying T-Rex, who greets you when you arrive!

Fun for the whole family, this self-guided tour makes its way along a graveled path that is wheelchair and stroller accessible. Dogs are welcome, as well.

Located 12.2 miles south of Port Orford on Hwy 101

Admission:

Adults:	$12.00
Children: (3 to 12 yrs)	$8.00
Seniors: (60+)	$10.00
Ages 2 and Under:	Free

Prehistoric Gardens
36848 Hwy 101
Port Orford, OR 97465
541-332-4463

- Open: Spring & Fall – 10:00 a.m. to 5:00 p.m., Summer: 9:00 a.m. to 6:00 p.m. – Call for winter hours.

www.Discover-Oregon.com

GOLD BEACH, OR

 ☐ **Jerry's Rogue Jets**

Imagine flying atop a scenic Oregon river at over 40 mph with 100' high rock walls whipping by so close to the boat that you're sure you could reach out and touch them. Breaking out into an open stretch of water, your guide hits the gas as the boat begins to dive left, suddenly careening into a 180 degree spin, followed by a huge splash of water...and everybody aboard bursting into laughter and applause.

Oregon Coast adventure awaits on a jet boat ride up the scenic Rogue River from Gold Beach, OR. Choose from a menu of three family-friendly trips, all with a knowledgeable and skilled river guide who will provide a narrated overview of the river, its plentiful flora and  fauna, the impressive geologic features you'll pass through, and stories about famous movies shot on the river itself, all with a boatload of thrills and laughs along the way. Keep your eyes out for bears and deer on the bank, Bald Eagles flying overhead, Great Blue Herons nesting in the fir trees, and a salmon or two tugging at the lines of fishermen as you pass by.

Season: May 1st through mid-October

Tours:

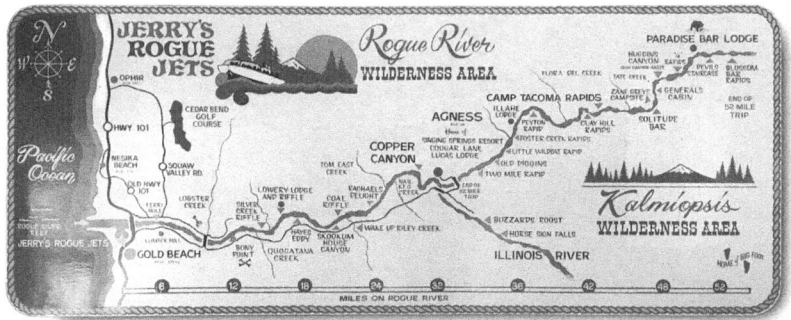

- **64 Mile Historic Mail Route**

    A casual and scenic 64 mile round-trip jet boat excursion without any whitewater. Plan on 4.5 hours, which includes a 1 hour meal stop at Agness, OR, on the river. The jet boat fare does not include the cost of your meal.

    Departure Times:

    - May 15 to June 30 - 9:30 a.m.
    - July 1 to August 31 – 9:30 a.m. & 3:00 p.m.
    - September 1 to Oct. 15 – 9:30 a.m.

    Fares:

    - Adult: $50
    - Child (4 to 11): $25.00
    - 3 And under: Free

- **80 Mile Whitewater Excursion**

    Perfect for those who want a bit of whitewater adventure. You'll pass over and through 6 different sets of rapids along your 80 mile round-trip excursion. Plan on stopping periodically along the way for photo opportunities, to watch a fisherman battle a salmon, view and learn about the wildlife, and more. This trip takes 4.75 hours, and stops for a 1 hour meal break, which is not included in the price of your trip.

    Departure Times:

    - June 15 to June 30 - 12:00 p.m.
    - July 1 to August 31 - 8:45 a.m., 12:00 p.m. & 2:15 p.m.
    - September 1 to September 15 - 12:00 p.m.

    Fares:

    - Adult: $70
    - Child (4 to 11): $35.00
    - 3 And under: Free

- **104 Mile Wilderness Whitewater**

    It's a full day of whitewater adventure on the majestic Rogue River! The 104 mile round-trip takes boaters into the 'Wild" section of the river, which can be reached only by rafting, hiking, and jet boating. You'll learn about the history of the river along the way from your skilled guide, as well as race through the canyons while keeping an eye out for bears, river otters, osprey, bald eagles and more.

    Departure Times:

    - May 1 to June 30 - 9:00 a.m.
    - July 1 to August 31 - 8:15 a.m. & 11:30 a.m.
    - September 1 to September 30 - 9:00 a.m.

Fares:

- Adult: $95
- Child (4 to 11): $45.00
- 3 And under: Free

Plan to arrive and check in at least 15 to 30 minutes prior to your departure time.

What to Wear:

You'll want to dress in layers, especially during the spring season of May through early June, when the weather is less stable and the water is cooler, as well as the month of September, when the water is warmer, but the air is cooler in the afternoons. With the coastal fog, you will find you're pretty well bundled up when you depart Gold Beach, but once you're up river 15 miles or so, you may find yourself in the warm sunshine. Keep in mind, however, that while you may spend the afternoon in a t-shirt, you'll want as much warmth as you can muster during the last 10 miles downriver as you speed back into the coastal fog. Bring a hat, windbreaker, warm coat and wind pants *if it will be foggy upon your return to Gold Beach.* (Do not underestimate this!) Call Jerry's on the day of your trip to get a sense of the weather. Note that we've been splashed on the jet boats, but not soaked. That doesn't mean you won't be, however.

During the summer months, you can expect highs in the 80s and 90s, so typical summer attire is fine. *Be sure to bring sunscreen, sunglasses and water.* A hat is also advised, since you'll be in the sun for much of the time during the longer trips upriver.

 FYI, we found it beneficial to bring a small pair of binoculars for viewing wildlife. We were fortunate to spot bear cubs on the two trips we've taken.

Jerry's Rogue Jets
29985 Harbor Way
Gold Beach, OR 97444
800-451-3645

Note: For those wanting a bit more adventure, you have the option of staying overnight at Paradise Lodge 52 miles upriver. Bring an overnight bag with a change of clothes and sundries, and enjoy the ride upriver to the lodge, where you'll stay the night before catching the return boat back to Gold Beach the next day. We enjoyed the overnight stay, but we're hesitant to recommend it to others until Paradise Lodge fixes a problem they have with their cabins, and that is that their gas fireplaces vent exhaust out the front of the fireplace *directly into your room*, which makes your room smell a bit foul the entire time you're there, even if it is just the pilot light that is burning. Inquire with Jerry's Rogue Jets if you'd like to add this option to your 104 mile trip.

☐ Jerry's Rogue River Museum

After a thrilling day of adventure on Jerry's Rogue Jets, visit Jerry's Rogue River Museum, just across the parking lot. Here, you'll learn about the rich natural and cultural history of the Rogue River, its original inhabitants, and the early pioneers along the river, as well as the history of Jerry's Rogue Jets as it has operated through the years.

Jerry's Rogue River Museum
29880 Harbor Dr.
Gold Beach, OR 97444
541-247-9737

- Open: Monday through Saturday - 9:00 a.m. to 6:00 p.m., Sunday - 10:00 a.m. to 5:00 p.m. - Open until 9:00 p.m. during July and August.

The Isaac Lee Patterson Memorial Bridge

If you appreciate fine engineering and architecture mixed with Oregon history, then you'll enjoy the Isaac Lee Patterson Memorial Bridge.

Prior to the 1930s, travelers along the Oregon coast would have to cross major rivers and bays by ferryboat, which added considerable time to their trip as they waited for the ferry to return, then to board, and then to cross. If the weather was poor, the rivers flooded, or the ferryboat wasn't working, then they were at the mercy of time. Beginning in the early 1930s, highway engineer Conde McCullough designed and built a series of bridges along the length of the Oregon coast which eliminated this problem and eased travel burdens considerably. With seven impressive spans showcasing the Art Deco style of the period, the 1931 Isaac Lee Patterson Memorial bridge is one of the finest examples of Mr. McCullough's work.

Perhaps the best place to see the bridge during the morning hours, when the light comes from the east, is at Lex's Landing, just to the east of its northern end.

If you'd like to learn more about the engineering and construction of Oregon's coastal bridges, we highly recommend the book *Lifting Oregon Out of the Mud – Building the Oregon Coast Highway*, by Joe R. Blakely. Look for it at gift shops and bookstores along the coast.

☐ Curry Historical Society Museum

A small museum on Hwy 101 dedicated to preserving the history of Oregon's south coast and Gold Beach regions through a collection of interesting and well-curated displays.

Admission: Adults: $2.00, Children under 16: $0.50

> Curry Historical Society Museum
> 29419 Ellensburg (On Hwy 101)
> Gold Beach, OR 97444
> 541-247-9396

- Open: Tuesday through Saturday – 10:00 a.m. to 4:00 p.m. – Closed during January

☐ Cape Sebastian Viewpoint & Trail

Turn right off of Hwy 101 and take the short road through a Sitka Spruce forest to the south parking lot. Take the 1.5 mile trail here out to the cape to enjoy a stunning panoramic view, and then continue down to the beach at Hunter's Cove. The Cape Sebastian Viewpoint trail is approximately 6.2 miles south of Gold Beach.

SAMUEL H. BOARDMAN
STATE SCENIC CORRIDOR

Entering

Samuel H. Boardman

State Scenic Corridor

Stretching for 12 linear miles along the southern Oregon Coast, just north of the California border, is the Samuel H. Boardman State Scenic Corridor. Honoring its namesake, whom is widely recognized as the father of the Oregon State Parks system, this collection of 11 scenic viewpoints and points of interest encapsulates some of the most scenic and dramatic coastline of the entire Oregon coast and features stunning vistas, rugged shorelines, sandy beaches, and more. In addition, most points make excellent locations from which to spot whales as they journey north and south.

There are actually two different Samuel H. Boardman State Scenic Corridors; one that visitors see from the pullout or parking lot at each destination, and the other which they experience after taking the brief hike found at most locations. We strongly encourage you to hike beyond the parking areas and down the different trails so as to enjoy a much more dramatic and awe-inspiring coastline. Note: In the descriptions that follow, you'll see two numbers reflecting our rating for that site. The first rates the site based upon what you'll see from the parking area, and the second rates the same site, but after hiking the trail to a nearby viewpoint, meadow, or beach. As you'll see in all cases, it's much more rewarding to leave the parking lot and explore the (usually) short trails.

☐ **Stop #1** - Arch Rock – 6 / **10** - (Mile 344.8)

Offering one of the best ocean views in the Scenic Corridor, Arch Rock Point is reached via a short paved path that leads to beautiful views of sea stacks and Arch Rock itself.

☐ **Stop #2** - Spruce Island & Secret Beach – 2/8 (Mile 345.0)

Spruce Island, Secret Beach, and Thunder Rock Cove all have roadside pullouts, beginning with Spruce Island on the north end, at Mile 345.0. Park here and take the trail south through a Sitka Spruce forest to a close up look at a collection of large sea stacks, and then either continue south on the trail to Secret Beach, which is very scenic, or return to your car and proceed to the parking area for Secret Beach at Mile 345.3. Keep an eye out for some unofficial yet very handy hand-drawn maps near the trailheads.

☐ **Stop #3** - Thunder Rock Cove – 0 / **10** - (Mile 345.8)

Just south of Secret Beach is the Thunder Rock Cove Viewpoint. Take the short dirt trail, which begins on the northern end of the parking lot, to the cove. Here, you'll find outstanding views of the rugged coastline and dramatic rock formations below.

☐ **Stop #4** - Natural Bridges – 0 / **7** - (Mile 346.0)

A short paved trail and wooden walkway quickly takes you to one of the more well-known features of the Scenic Corridor, the Natural Bridges.

☐ **Stop #5** - North Island – 0 / **6** - (Mile 347.4)

Find the trail on the south end of the parking area and make your way through the forest before breaking out into an overgrown "meadow", which leads down into a bowl, terminating at a ledge high above the surf. Note that if it has rained recently, your pants

will get wet as you hike through all of the overgrowth.

☐ Stop #6 - Indian Sands – 3 / 6 - (Mile 348.6)

With Indian Sands, you'll hike ½ mile down to a collection of sandstone features high above the waterline. Note that the sand here isn't from the ocean, but instead from an exposed sandstone bluff above the high tide line.

☐ Stop #7 - Whaleshead Beach – 2 / 8 - (Mile 349.3)

Just before reaching the Whaleshead Beach RV Resort, turn right and make your way down a short and sometimes rough road to a large paved parking area with restrooms, and then follow the short trail from here to Whaleshead Beach, a long and beautiful

beach with sea stacks. Note, this road is sometimes impassable in large mobile homes, and it may take a little finesse to get your car down to the parking area. There is a sign recommending 4 wheel drive vehicles, but there was a Prius in the parking lot when we last arrived.

☐ Stop #8 - House Rock – 3 / 10 - (Mile 351.2)

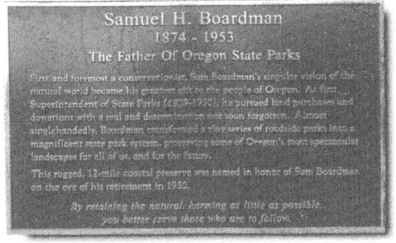

Simply drive to the parking area and climb 7 wide steps to a short paved path that leads to a 180+ degree panoramic view, dedicated to Samuel H. Boardman.

147

Stop #9 - Cape Ferrelo – **8** - (Mile 351.9)

Cape Ferrelo is a small viewpoint with a nice view, and look for wildflowers here in the spring. Note that the parking area is small, so there is no trailer turnaround available.

Stop #10 - Lone Ranch Picnic Area – **10** - (Mile 352.6)

This is a large open park with 10 picnic tables lining a short path to a long beach punctuated with sea stacks and piles of driftwood. You'll find easy access in and out of the large paved parking area.

BROOKINGS, OR

☐ Harris Beach State Park

At the northern end of Brookings is Harris Beach State Park. Located within the "Banana Belt" of Oregon, it offers warmer and more favorable weather than the rest of the coast during the winter months. Its long sandy beaches are interspersed with intriguing tide pools that make up one of Oregon's seven designated Marine Gardens, and just offshore you'll find an interesting collection of sea stacks, as well as Bird Island, the largest island off the Oregon Coast and home to over 100,000 nesting seabirds representing 11 species, including the Tufted Puffin. In addition, look for Gray Whales, California Sea Lions and other marine life while you're here.

☐ Brookings – Harbor Farmers Market

Open year-round, the Brookings-Harbor Farmers Market offers food, produce, baked goods, treats, locally crafted artwork, and more.

You'll find the market open every Wednesday and Saturday from 10:00 a.m. to 3:00 p.m.

Brookings - Harbor Farmers Market
15786 Hwy 101 South
Brookings, OR 97415

☐ Oregon Redwoods Trails #1106 & #1107

Located near the California Border, the Oregon Redwoods Trails #1106 & #1107 offer a hike amongst towering old-growth redwood trees, the only coast redwoods found in the Pacific Northwest. Combine the two trails to create a loop featuring interpretive panels describing the life cycle, fire history, and eco-systems of these majestic trees, growing at the northern limit of their range.

Directions: You'll find these two trails approximately 11 miles or ½ hour southeast of Brookings. From Brookings, follow Hwy 101 south approximately 5 miles to County Road 896 / Winchuck Road. Turn west onto Winchuck Road and follow this approximately 1.6 miles to Peavine Ridge Road / Forest Road 1101. Turn right here and then follow this sometimes challenging-to-drive dirt road 4 miles to its end, where you'll find the trailhead for these "must see" trails.

☐ Chetco Valley Historical Society Museum

Housed in a former stagecoach stop built in 1857, the Chetco Valley Museum showcases the story of the Chetco River and its native and early pioneers. Inside, you'll find rooms depicting the lives of eras past through displays of typical household items, hundreds of photos, cases of old cameras, kitchen items, World War II artifacts, and more.

Chetco Valley Historical Society Museum
15461 Museum Road
Brookings, OR 97415
541-469-6651

- Open: Saturday and Sunday – 12:00 p.m. to 4:00 p.m.

NOW ENJOY AN OREGON COAST ROAD TRIP!

Oregon Road Trips – Oregon Coast Edition

If you enjoyed your day or weekend visit to the Oregon Coast, then you'll love exploring all the grandeur of Oregon's dramatic coastline during an adventurous 9-day road trip from Astoria south to Brookings. You'll journey along Oregon's beautiful Highway 101 as you discover countless scenic beaches, tour historic lighthouses, wander through quaint beach towns, watch whales spouting just off shore, ride in the cab of a 1925 steam locomotive, eat tasty Dungeness Crab fresh off the boat...or catch your own, stay in historic hotels, explore unique shops, meet friendly people and so much more!

Your perfect 9-day Oregon Coast road trip awaits and it's already planned for you, from start to finish!

Available Now at Retailers
Throughout Oregon and Online

A NORTHEAST OREGON ROAD TRIP!

Oregon Road Trips – Northeast Edition

Now discover Northeast Oregon's scenic backroads and byways by day, *while staying in historic hotels by night!*

With our *Oregon Road Trips – Northeast Edition* guide, you'll explore the scenic beauty of Northeast Oregon while you ride aboard a historic steam train, wander Oregon ghost towns, ascend in a cable tram to over 8,000', stay at the 1907 Balch Hotel, board the Sumpter Valley Dredge, explore Cottonwood Canyon, ride the rails on a 2-seater, explore unique shops, eat at great restaurants, meet friendly people and so much more!

An adventurous Northeast Oregon road trip awaits, and it's already planned for you!

Available Now at Retailers
Throughout Oregon and Online

AND ANOTHER GREAT ROAD TRIP AWAITS!

Oregon Road Trips – Southeast Edition

Ready for a remote Oregon adventure? Then you'll love *Oregon Road Trips – Southeast Edition.* As with all of our road trip guides, you'll simply turn each page as you motor along and choose which points of interest to stop at and explore during your day's journey, *all while making your way toward that evening's lodging in a historic Oregon hotel.*

You'll drive to the top of 9,734' Steens Mountain, stay in the 1923 Frenchglen Hotel, explore the remote Leslie Gulch, see how stage coaches are built, dig for fossils, hike "Crack in the Ground", look for wild Mustangs, eat at a truly unique and remote Oregon restaurant, marvel at the geologic wonders of the Journey Through Time Scenic Byway and so much more!

Available Now at Retailers
Throughout Oregon and Online

EXPLORE
SOUTHWEST OREGON!

Oregon Road Trips – Southwest Edition

Another Oregon adventure is already planned out for you!

Visit 13 historic covered bridges, spend a night in Crater Lake Lodge, discover a vintage aircraft museum, enjoy a play in Ashland, explore deep into the Oregon Caves, wander an Oregon ghost town, see some of Oregon's most beautiful waterfalls, tour the Applegate Wine Trail, and so much more on your 9-day road trip through Southwest Oregon. As with our other Oregon Road Trip books, you'll simply motor along while you discover Oregon, *and finish each night at a unique historic hotel!*

Available Now at Retailers
Throughout Oregon and Online

DISCOVER THE
COLUMBIA RIVER GORGE!

Oregon Road Trips –
Columbia River Gorge Edition

Journey along the Historic Columbia River Highway deep into the Columbia River Gorge, where you'll spend five days seeing the Gorge's majestic waterfalls, flying in a vintage 2-seater biplane, hiking through the historic Mosier Tunnels, stepping into the void on an exciting zip line tour, walking amidst the Gorge's beautiful spring wildflowers, finding your next book at Oregon's oldest bookstore, and even spotting Giraffes, Zebras, Camels, Ostriches and more!

Your Columbia River Gorge road trip awaits, and it's already planned for you!

Available Now at Retailers
Throughout Oregon and Online

WHALE WATCHING ON THE OREGON COAST

Our thanks to Tiffany Boothe of Oregon State Parks & Recreation, as well as VisitTheOregonCoast.com for this article.

Whale watching is a year-round activity on the Oregon Coast with gray whales by far the most commonly seen. Whale watching is not difficult, but a few tips make it easier. Any location with an ocean view may yield whale sightings, and morning light with the sun at your back is best. First locate whale spouts with your naked eye; then focus more closely with binoculars. For an even closer view, try whale watching from a charter boat. And some people prefer the view from above—from an airplane or helicopter. Both charter boats and air services are available (and listed here). And, of course, calmer days are best, whether by land, sea, or air.

Gray Whale Migration

Gray whales migrate South from their feeding grounds in the Bering and Chukchi seas around Alaska from mid-December through January. They are heading to their breeding grounds in Baja California, Mexico, where warm-water lagoons become nurseries for expectant mothers. Then from late March to June the whales migrate north back to Alaska. On each trip, approximately 18,000 gray whales pass close to the Oregon Coast.

On the trip down, these giant mammals head South on a direct course, move quickly, and mostly stay about 5 miles offshore. At their peak, about 30 whales pass by each hour. Coming back, the whales travel much more leisurely and stay closer to shore—within a half mile is not unusual. The non-breeding males and females lead the way back with some early birds starting in late February. They may even pass stragglers still heading south. The northward migration continues at a slower pace and mothers with young don't usually appear until May.

Resident Gray Whales in Summer

Some gray whales do not continue on to Alaskan waters but stay off the coast of Oregon between June and November. These part-time residents number about 200. About 60 whales are seen repeatedly off the central coast and have been photographed and identified. Of these, about 40 hang out between Lincoln City and Newport each year because that seems to be what the food supply will support.

Whale Watching Spoken Here Program

Each year peak migration times coincide with people's vacation times. The *Whale Watching Spoken Here* program takes advantage of this coincidence with three weeks of assisted whale watching: the first is the week between Christmas and New Year's, the second is during the last week in March, and the third is the last week of August through the first Monday in September. The summer whale watch locations are those along the central coast and focus on the part-time resident whales. During each whale-watch week hundreds of volunteers man 26 sites along the coast from Ilwaco, Washington to Crescent City, California.

Spy Hopping and Breaching Behavior

The two whale behaviors that get people excited are spy hopping—where the head sticks straight up out of the water—and breaching—where 1/2 to 3/4 of the body length comes up out of the water and falls on its side or back causing a tremendous splash.

Where to Spot Whales

From north to south, here are 23 *Whale Watching Spoken Here* sites. With or without a volunteer to assist, these are the best locations along the coast to spot whales.

1. Ecola State Park
2. Neahkahnie Mountain Historic Marker Turnout on Highway 101
3. Cape Meares State Scenic Viewpoint
4. Cape Lookout State Park – 2.5 mile hike to the tip of the Cape
5. Cape Kiwanda at Pacific City
6. Inn at Spanish Head - Lobby on the 10th floor
7. Boiler Bay State Scenic Viewpoint
8. The Whale Watching Center/Depoe Bay Sea Wall
9. Rocky Creek State Scenic Viewpoint
10. Cape Foulweather
11. Devil's Punchbowl State Natural Area
12. Yaquina Head Outstanding Natural Area
13. Don Davis City Park
14. Cape Perpetua Interpretive Center
15. Cook's Chasm Turnout
16. Umpqua Lighthouse, near Umpqua Lighthouse State Park
17. Shore Acres State Park
18. Face Rock Wayside State Scenic Viewpoint
19. Cape Blanco Lighthouse, near Cape Blanco State Park
20. Battle Rock Wayfinding Point, Port Orford
21. Cape Sebastian
22. Cape Ferrelo
23. Harris Beach State Park, Brookings, Oregon

Whale Watching by Sea and Air

Whale watching is better in the spring through fall months when the seas and skies offer smoother conditions.

Charterboats:

- Rockaway Beach - Linda Sue III Charters & Troller, 503-355-3419
- Garibaldi - D&D Charters (spring through fall), 800-900-HOOK (4665)
- Depoe Bay – Whale Research EcoExcursions – 541-912-6743 - www.OregonWhales.com
- Depoe Bay - Tradewinds Charters, 800-445-8730

- Depoe Bay - Dockside Charters, also have Zodiacs, 800-733-8915
- Newport - Marine Discovery Tours (spring through fall), 65-foot Discovery, 800-903-BOAT (2628)
- Newport - Bayfront Charters, 800-828-8777
- Newport - Sea Gull Charters, 800-865-7441
- Newport Tradewinds, 800-676-7819
- Newport Marina Store and Charters, South Beach, 541-867-4470
- Charleston - Betty Kay Charters, 800-752-6303
- Brookings - Tidewind Sportfishing, 800-799-0337

Scenic & Whale-Watch Flights:

Most flights carry from one to three passengers. Rates vary and reservations are recommended but not always required. All flights are dependent upon the weather.

- Twiss Air Service/Astoria Flight Center, one to three passengers, Astoria 503-861-1222
- Tillamook Air Tours, one to four passengers, 503-842-1942
- Florence Aviation, one passenger, Florence 541-997-8069
- Crosswind Air Tours, two or three passengers (minimum two), Florence 541-997-8069
- Coos Aviation, one to three passengers, North Bend 541-756-5181
- Frank's Flight Service, one to three passengers, Bandon 541-347-2022

www.Discover-Oregon.com

WE RECOMMEND...

Lifting Oregon Out of the Mud – Building the Oregon Coast Highway

If you'd like to learn more about the engineering and construction of Oregon's impressive coastal bridges, we highly recommend the book *Lifting Oregon Out of the Mud – Building the Oregon Coast Highway*, by Joe R. Blakely. Look for it at gift shops and bookstores along the coast, as well as online. www.Powells.com

Les Schwab Tire Centers

If you're on the road and have a flat tire, brake issues or a similar problem, we highly recommend the very helpful folks at your nearby Les Schwab Tire Center. You'll find 10 locations along the Oregon Coast.

Are You a Disney Fan?

Enjoy three great books that reveal 100s of hidden secrets, which the Disney Imagineers have purposely hidden for park guests to find and enjoy; 1) *The Hidden Secrets & Stories of Disneyland*, 2) *Disneyland In-Depth*, and 3) *The Hidden Secrets & Stories of Walt Disney World*.

Available online and at the world-renowned Walt Disney Family Museum and the Walt Disney Hometown Museum.

50718128R00095

Made in the USA
Columbia, SC
11 February 2019